FIRED

DeliVita
LIFE IS SO ENDLESSLY DELICIOUS

Contents

ABOUT THE AUTHORS

Pioneers of the American barbecue scene in the UK since 2010, Jon & Ben created Grillstock, the original barbecue and music festival, which drew 20,000 meat fans annually to their weekend of meat, music and mayhem. They also co-authored an Amazon best-selling barbecue cookbook of the same name. Last year they worked together on *Beer Craft – The no-nonsense guide to enjoying craft beer at home.*

Their passion for live-fire cooking doesn't stop at barbecues, though. The pair have been cooking in wood ovens for over a decade and have now collated more than a hundred of their favourite recipes in *Fired.*

A BIG THANKS TO . . .

From Jon:
Marie-Louise, Noah and Jake for being as excited as I am about this book. Mum & Dad, *grazie mille* for taking us all to Masseria Ionna in Italy every year and for bringing me up with a huge passion for food.

From Ben:
Esme, Beau, Horace and Roxy for helping me test the recipes.

From us both:
Joe and Liv at Delivita (www.delivita.co.uk) for the awesome kit. You guys know how to make a su-perb wood oven! Marcus Bawdon – for all the help and advice on everything wood-oven related. And for the kick-ass pizza dough recipe. Jen, George, Jules and Clare, Morgan, Jude and Samuel for the endless pizza-testing sessions – you guys are troopers. Cyrus for eating all the pizza. Sim-ba for keeping us company on photo days. Romy Gill for the sublime Indian dishes – your new cookbook will be a best seller! Ruth Hickson (www.ruthhickson.com) for the fabulous illustrations. Adam, Nithya, Hannah and the team at Little, Brown – the best publishers ever.

INTRODUCTION

I first cooked in a proper wood-fired oven in the summer of 2009. A *masseria*, a new family country home, had been built in Puglia, in the south of Italy, with a huge, almost catering-size, olive-wood burning pizza oven in the garden.

The highlight of our trips there included the whole family rolling up their sleeves for regular pizza nights. One person would be in charge of getting the fire in the oven going, another would make the dough, someone else would head out for toppings and the unlucky one would get to wash up afterwards. When everything was ready to go, we'd all gather at a big outdoor table and take it in turns to cook pizzas that would then be shared out. Kids usually went first, topping their pizza bases with dollops of pomodoro sauce and unceremoniously dumping little fistfuls of sweetcorn over the top. Then came the adults, getting more and more ambitious and creative with their toppings as the wine flowed and the candles were lit.

Initially, we focused solely on cooking pizzas: building the best fire, learning when to add more logs and when to ease back, understanding when the fire was just right for pizza making, refining our dough recipe and playing around with toppings and different cheeses.

But with such an abundance of wonderful fresh ingredients in southern Italy and inspired by creative wood-oven dishes featured on local restaurant menus, it wasn't long until we started getting more and more adventurous with our dishes. Initially, it was trays of peppers or courgettes, drizzled with olive oil and a scattering of herbs and sea salt, then local *orata* (sea bream) plucked from the sea that morning and stuffed to the gills with fresh herbs and lemons. It wasn't long before the oven was in use all day, with pizzas for lunch and complete meals comprising roast potatoes and whole slow-roasted joints of meat for dinner heading for the oven, and then bread baking away in the dying ashes for the next day.

Cooking in a wood-fired oven is easy. There are no dials, switches or thermostats. You can't set it to 220°C and forget about it. But that's half the charm – it's a simpler way of cooking, and once you understand how your wood oven behaves, it all suddenly makes sense. Learn to understand the various cooking stages, to love the ritual of lighting it and slowly building the fire.

Wood ovens bring people together – they are a very sociable, communal way to cook and eat. They make food taste great and, best of all, you get to play with fire!

Jon

WHAT IS THIS BOOK?

FIRED WILL HELP YOU MAKE THE MOST OF YOUR NEW WOOD-FIRED OVEN.

A decade ago, if you wanted a wood oven in your garden you had no option but to pay thousands for a professionally installed, imported authentic Italian brick-built wood oven. It would be the size of a small shed and built to last generations. Sure, cooking in it would be an absolute delight, but it needed 3 hours of burning logs to heat up to the right temperature and then, unless you were a trained Italian *pizzaiolo*, controlling the temperature would be near impossible, meaning you either cremated anything in seconds or nothing ever cooked.

But in the blink of an eye we're suddenly in the midst of a wood-oven revolution. The new generation of pizza ovens are small and portable; they are often colourful, modern and striking in their design. They look just as at home in a backyard in Dulwich as they do on a balcony in Edinburgh, or in a leafy garden in the Cotswolds. And because they take up less space than an average barbecue, they can be thrown in the boot of the car to take camping or for a picnic.

The fact is, wood ovens are incredibly versatile. Clearly, they make better pizzas than ones made in a domestic oven, but they are terrific at so many things: whole Sunday roast joints, trays of roasted vegetables, one-pot stews, breads, desserts and so much more besides.

Fired offers everything from advice on first setting up your wood oven and managing the fire, easy recipes for the first-time user, through to interesting and exciting dishes for the more adventurous wood-fired cook.

THE BASICS

ESSENTIAL KIT

PEELS

A peel is the name given to the paddle-like tools that are used to slide pizzas and other dishes in and out of ovens.

I recommend two peels: a wooden one for sliding uncooked pizzas and breads into the oven, as the dough is less likely to stick to wood; and a metal one for fetching them out again. The metal one is also good for most other things.

PIG FLIPPER

A pig flipper is a metal rod with a savage-looking hook on the end. Sounds a bit gruesome, but nothing beats it for moving large cuts of meat or steaks around a grill or inside a wood oven. I have two sizes: one is converted from an old golf club with the head sawn off and a hook welded on instead – this is my favourite one; the other is much smaller, but is very useful in higher spaces or with small pieces of meat.

My trusty pig flipper is my right-hand man whenever I'm cooking outdoors. Aside from its intended purpose of moving meat around quickly, it is just right for moving logs, embers, coals, dishes, etc. around the oven. Its long handle helps protect your hands from the heat too.

BRUSHES

I have two different brushes for my wood oven. One is a harsh wire metal brush like you'd use to clean a barbecue, except with a longer handle. I use this to clean down the floor of the oven while cooking to keep any burnt food or embers out of the way. The second brush has long, soft bristles that get into all the corners. I use this for sweeping out the ashes once everything has cooled down the next day.

OVEN GLOVES – BARBECUE ONES

You know the flameproof suits that racing drivers wear? You can get oven gloves made out of that stuff too. How awesome is that? They're heatproof well up to and beyond the crazy temperature your wood oven gets to (some up to 800°C), yet still remain flexible and nimble enough to easily use while cooking. Opt for a pair that has silicon grips on the palms and also look out for ones that have long cuffs. Mine come halfway to my elbows.

Owning a decent pair of heatproof gloves makes wood-oven cooking so much easier! Turning or moving big crock pots full of hot liquid is really difficult with anything except your hands. Get online now and order yourself a pair. The Weber barbecue ones are very good.

Alternatively, you can pick up a pair of welding gloves at your local DIY store. I have been known to use thick leather gardening gloves at a pinch, but they only offer a few seconds of protection.

One word of advice: make sure the gloves are not damp or wet when you use them or the heat will transfer right through! You can get waterproof silicone ones if you are clumsy or want that extra peace of mind.

TWO THERMOMETERS

Yes, I know ancient Italians never had two thermometers and yet managed to cook delicious food, but I am trying to make your life easy as well as make you look good in front of your friends. You need one thermometer to tell how hot your oven is and a second, different type of thermometer to gauge the internal temperature of your food.

A point-and-shoot laser thermometer is spot on for outdoor cooking. Aim it at the floor of the oven a few inches from the mouth, not directly at the fire. When your laser thermometer arrives you will spend the first three days ascertaining the temperature of virtually everything in your house, including pets and children. Don't worry, this won't last.

The other type of thermometer I recommend is an instant-read, probe variety to poke into various meats to find out how well done they are. Never again serve overcooked steak or undercooked chicken. This toy ensures perfect doneness. Where relevant I have added the internal temperatures to aim for in each recipe.

BARBECUE TONGS

Get yourself a couple of pairs of good-quality, heatproof tongs (I like the OXO brand with the silicon handles).

NITRILE GLOVES

These are the blue plastic gloves you see restaurant kitchen staff wearing. They have to wear blue ones in case a bit gets into the food, but you don't have to. You can wear any colour you think looks cool. Personally, I like the black ones. A box of nitrile gloves should be a permanent addition to your outdoor cooking toolkit. Unless you have built a big fancy outdoor kitchen it's unlikely you will have access to hot running water to wash your hands. Nitrile gloves mean you can do all the messy jobs, handle raw meat and cooked meat alike, without any worry of cross-contamination.

FOIL

Foil is ever-present when I'm manning the wood oven. I use it to cover up cooked dishes while they're resting, to seal in moisture in slow-cook dishes or to cover and protect dishes from the heat if they are getting a bit toastier than planned. Go for thick catering foil. Costco is best. See page 84 for more on foil.

FIRELIGHTERS

Most firelighters contain paraffin or other chemicals to get the fire going quickly. You need to avoid these in your wood oven as the chemicals can easily leach into the oven floor and taint future food cooked there. For that very reason, don't use lighter fuel either! You wouldn't want your pizza base tasting like lighter fuel, would you? Instead, opt for flamers. They are a small bird's nest of shredded wood that goes up in no time. They're also handy to light and throw into the fire if you need a spark.

3-FOOT COPPER PIPE

This is a suggestion from my friend Marcus who runs CountryWoodSmoke. He has a length of copper pipe by his side to use to blow into the fire when it needs a little help. When you throw a new log on, it sometimes smoulders for ages and needs a bit of a draft. This avoids getting a faceful of hot embers!

HOW TO LIGHT THE FIRE

Gather together your firelighters and about 8–10 pieces of kindling. These should be 15–20cm long and no more than 1cm thick.

Place a firelighter or two in the centre of the oven and put a piece of kindling lengthways either side of it. Now place two more pieces of kindling on top, running the opposite direction (kind of like a hollow Jenga tower).

Finally, add two more pieces of kindling on top, facing the same direction as the first two. You should now have a couple of firelighters at the bottom and a small tower, three sticks tall, of kindling. Continue until your tower is 4–5 sticks high.

Light the firelighter and allow the fire to catch. When it is well on its way, you can start to add small pieces of split logs: around 20cm long and 2–3cm wide is good.

Allow the fire to build further and start increasing the thickness of the split logs you are adding until you have a good hot fire going. At this point start adding your cooking logs (rather than kindling) and bring the temperature to a consistent 300–400°C.

Logs for cooking should be 8–10cm wide and the number you need to maintain the temperature will vary according to the size of your oven. The bigger the oven, the longer it will take to reach cooking temperature and the more logs you'll have to feed it per hour.

Remember to add logs while the fire is still going well. If you let it die down too much (even if the oven remains hot) it will be harder for the logs to catch fire.

Once you have a controlled fire and good consistent temperature going, you can push the fire to the back or side of the oven, brush over the floor and get cooking!!!

WOODS

One of the most important considerations in wood-oven cooking is your choice of fuel. Some wood types burn hot and fast, others burn cooler but for longer. Some light in an instant, others take more work. Importantly, some will add a delicious flavour to your food, but be warned: others can impart a nasty bitterness.

The length of time the wood has been stored since cutting is also very important. Fresh logs still 'wet' with sap will be hard to light. Once lit, they will smoulder and smoke their way through. We're looking for a clean, efficient fire in our wood oven, so try to find logs that have been seasoned somewhere dry for at least a year. A slightly more expensive option is kiln-dried logs. As it sounds, the wood is placed in a large oven and dried out as much as possible. Kiln-dried logs light well and burn consistently and cleanly.

You can mix up the wood types you are using. Certain recipes lend themselves to a big hit of smokiness, whereas quite the opposite can be true with others.

ONE GOLDEN RULE IS TO AVOID BURNING ANY KIND OF SOFT WOOD SUCH AS PINE. THEY ARE VERY RESINOUS AND WHILE THEY CATCH FIRE QUICKLY, THEY WILL GIVE OFF A THICK, BLACK, ACRID SMOKE AND NASTY FLAVOURS.

The remaining suitable wood types can be divided into two types: hard woods and fruit woods. I like to use the hard woods as my base fuel to generate the consistent heat I need to cook, then lay in some small chunks of fruit wood about the size of a fist around the edge of the embers to give an aromatic smoky note when required. Don't use wood chips or smoking wood powders as they will burn up too quickly.

For fuel, use: Oak, silver birch, beech, ash, alder, olive.
For an extra hit of flavour, use: Apple, pear, walnut, cherry.

MANAGE THE FIRE

Once your fire is away and you are happy with the temperature, the next step is to keep the temperature consistent. Test the temperature often using a digital thermometer and add a log as and when needed.

I keep a pile of logs in varying sizes handy when cooking: little bits of kindling to help reignite a smouldering fire; small 8–10cm wide logs for keeping a mellow fire on the go; and larger 20cm wide logs for achieving higher-temperature cooking.

If the size of your oven allows, it's useful to lay a few logs near the entrance to the oven, or even inside the oven on the opposite side to the fire. This will heat them up and they'll ignite much more quickly than cold logs.

COOLING DOWN

It's quite easy to overshoot your intended temperature – one log too many and all of a sudden your oven is 100°C hotter than you want it to be. If you are in no hurry, then one option is to just wait until the oven has cooled down. Other options are to mop over the floor of the oven using a wet cloth on the end of your pig flipper (or similar). You can also spread the fire out on the oven floor to burn through a bit quicker, then pile the embers back up against the wall to cook.

CURING THE OVEN

Some wood ovens made from clay will need to be cured before you can use them. While the ovens are made of a heatproof clay, there may still be some moisture present from when they were made, and this needs to be dried out slowly – a process called 'curing'.

The curing process is really easy: just light a small fire that burns at a low temperature inside the oven for 3–4 hours, starting at 50°C and working up to about 200°C. Remember that your pizza oven may well be hitting and exceeding 500°C once it is firing on all cylinders. To cure a wood oven, follow these simple steps:

1) Light a firelighter with a few small bits of kindling built in a tower over it towards the rear of the oven. Once it is going well, add another couple of pieces of kindling.

2) Keep monitoring the temperature and continue adding small bits of kindling as and when required.

3) After 3–4 hours, allow the fire to die down and let the oven cool completely. If you see quite a bit of moisture come out, you may want to repeat the curing process one more time before you get your oven up to full cruising altitude.

Note: **If your oven has got wet or hasn't been used for a while, it's worth running a curing session for a few hours prior to building the temperature up with a larger hot fire.**

COOKING IN A WOOD OVEN

THE VERY NATURE OF WOOD OVENS MEANS AIMING FOR SPECIFIC COOKING TEMPERATURES IS IMPRACTICAL.

WE'RE COOKING WITH LIVE FIRE AND EVERY SINGLE LOG BURNS UNIQUELY.

ADDITIONALLY, THE OUTSIDE AMBIENT TEMPERATURE CHANGES; EVERYONE'S OVEN COOKS DIFFERENTLY, AND UNLESS WOOD IS ADDED FREQUENTLY, THE TEMPERATURE WILL ALWAYS BE DROPPING OFF; WE HAVE NO THERMOSTATS, HEATING ELEMENTS OR OTHER TECHNOLOGICAL ADVANCES TO HELP US CONTROL OR MAINTAIN THE TEMPERATURE.

INSTEAD, IT IS EASIER TO LOOK AT A SERIES OF FAIRLY BROAD TEMPERATURE BANDS TO COOK AT.

ONCE YOU'VE COOKED WITH YOUR OWN OVEN A HANDFUL OF TIMES, ACHIEVING AND MAINTAINING THESE BANDS WILL BECOME SECOND NATURE.

SCREAMING HOT
300–450°C

This is pizza-cooking temperature. The flames are licking the roof. Your oven is as hot as it gets and most other foods will char and burn within seconds.

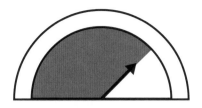

SIZZLING HOT
220–300°C

Still a few flames, but not as aggressive as screaming hot. This is perfect for steaks and other dishes that need a hard and fast cooking time.

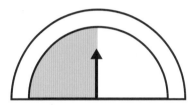

ROASTING
160–200°C

Very few or no flames now, but with bright, hot, strong burning embers. This is about the same temperature as domestic kitchen ovens cook at. A great all-round temperature for most dishes.

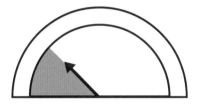

LOW AND SLOW
120–160°C

Dying embers with a log added very occasionally to stop the fire from going out. Perfect for stews, slow-cook joints of meat and overnight slow bakes.

DOOR OPEN OR CLOSED?

Most pizza ovens come with a door, allowing you to cut off the oxygen and insulate the oven. This gives off a great ambient heat and is perfect for baking breads and for slow overnight cooks. Rake the embers out over the base of the oven for even better ambient heat. For anything other than bread or slow cooking, leave the door open.

TURN OFTEN

Unlike your kitchen oven, the heat in a wood oven comes mainly from one direction. Sure, the base pumps out heat and the domed roof reflects heat back down, but we have a log fire sitting back there. Take care to rotate your dishes and trays in the oven regularly. Stir often and be mindful that whatever side is closest to that fire is going to cook (or burn) quicker than the side you can see!

COOKING KIT

It's useful to have a few different oven-friendly cooking vessels so you can make the most of your oven. Don't be too precious about the look of your wood-oven cookware; it's going to get scuffed, blackened, scorched and roughed up the very first time you use it. It's half the charm!

Anything cast iron, stainless steel, copper or enamel will work well. Don't use anything with plastic or wooden handles. Importantly, make sure anything you buy fits through the door of your oven!

CAST-IRON SKILLET PANS

These are one of the most versatile and useful bits of kit, surely one of the reasons they are so popular in restaurant kitchens! Get a variety of sizes about 3cm deep with a decently long cast-iron handle. You'll use these more than anything!

CAST-IRON SIZZLER

Similar to the skillet pan, only flat, this is great for searing meats and other 'flash-sizzle' dishes. Essentially a cast-iron tray with a handle.

CASSEROLE DISH

An enamelled cast-iron casserole dish is great for roasting one-pot dishes and slow cooking. Don't go too big as it gets really heavy once full, making it tricky to easily slide in and out of the oven. Some recipes call for the dish to be covered, so buy crockpots with lids.

DUTCH OVEN

Similar to a casserole dish but with the addition of a thick, flat lid, the idea being that you can pile coals and embers on top to help distribute the heat evenly. Watch out for weight!

BAKING TRAYS OR DISHES

Shallow baking trays are perfect for roasting just about anything.

STAINLESS STEEL BOWLS

I like to use breakfast cereal-size bowls for quickly heating bastes, melting butters, and bringing small amounts of sauces or liquids to the boil. They can be moved around with a decent pair of tongs.

PIZZA TRAY

A flat, metal pizza-size tray is a good bit of kit if you are making lots and lots of pizzas or are having trouble sliding them around on the pizza peels.

MEAT TEMPERATURE CHART

Overcooking meat is just as bad as undercooking it. Invest in a decent instant-read probe thermometer and always know exactly where you are **(internal meat temperatures are shown in °C).**

BEEF AND LAMB		PORK CHOPS		CHICKEN & TURKEY	
Rare	54	Rare	54	Always	70
Chef's	57	Medium	60		
Medium	62	Chef's	65		
Well done	68+	Well done	68+		

SLOW-COOKED JOINTS OF MEAT	
Fall apart	92

STORING & CLEANING A WOOD OVEN

Store your wood oven in a shed or outdoor wood store that is sheltered from the rain but allows airflow.

Wood ovens are almost self-cleaning. Once you have finished cooking for the day, use a wire brush to scrub over where you have been cooking and rake the residual embers over the floor of the oven. Leave everything as is overnight (or until fully cooled), then use a soft brush to sweep out all the embers. That's it!

BRUNCH

FRENCH TOAST WITH COULIS

Try to get hold of the richest, butteriest brioche you can for this recipe.

Ingredients

Method

ROASTING – 160–200°C

Knob of butter

4 large egg yolks

100ml double cream

150ml milk

1 tbsp vanilla essence

½ tsp ground cinnamon

2 tbsp ice-cream sugar (see
below) or caster sugar

1 brioche loaf, cut into 3cm
thick slices (aim for 2
slices per person)

Crème fraîche, to serve

Icing sugar, to dust

Fresh mint leaves, to
garnish

FOR THE COULIS

250g fresh raspberries or
strawberries

250g caster sugar

Juice of 1 lemon

Start by making the coulis. Roughly chop the fruit, then transfer to a saucepan with the sugar and lemon juice. Heat in a medium wood oven until everything has melted down together. Push through a fine-mesh sieve if you don't like seeds, then allow to cool.

To make the French toast, preheat a skillet in a medium oven, then add the butter.

Whisk together the egg yolks, cream, milk, vanilla, cinnamon and ice-cream sugar, and tip into a shallow dish.

Dip each slice of brioche into the egg mixture for about 5 seconds, making sure the brioche doesn't get too soggy.

Gently lay the brioche in the skillet and return to the oven for 4–5 minutes. Flip and cook for a further 1–2 minutes.

Serve with a dollop of crème fraîche, a drizzle of coulis, a dusting of icing sugar and a few mint leaves.

Make ice-cream sugar in advance by adding 2–3 split vanilla pods to a jar of caster sugar. Shake every few days for about a week. The sugar (with the pods) will keep indefinitely. Just keep topping up the caster sugar with fresh stuff as you go.

Top tip If you find the brioche is getting too soggy during the dipping phase, you can first dry out the slices on a wire rack at the cool end of the oven for 5–10 minutes.

Serves
4

AMERICAN-STYLE PANCAKES

More and more I am getting into using US cups for home cooking. This recipe is a particularly easy one to remember the cup way!

Ingredients

120g plain flour (1 cup)

2 tbsp caster sugar

2 tsp baking powder

Pinch of salt

250ml milk (1 cup)

1 tbsp plain yoghurt

1 tsp vanilla extract

2 eggs

30g butter, melted

Oil for frying

Maple syrup, millionaire
    bacon (see page 25) and
    fresh berries, to serve

Method

ROASTING – 160-200°C

Mix all the dry ingredients together in a bowl.

Whisk all the wet ingredients in a separate bowl, then add to the dry ingredients and stir until combined.

Heat a skillet in the wood oven and wipe a little oil all over the pan using a paper towel, making sure there are no pools of oil.

When the oil is hot, spoon 2-3 tablespoons of the batter into the skillet. Cook for 1-2 minutes until the surface of the pancake starts to bubble, then carefully flip and cook for another 1-2 minutes.

Serve with maple syrup, millionaire bacon and fresh berries.

The yoghurt helps to activate the baking powder, making the pancakes particularly light and fluffy. If you make the batter a day (or even two) in advance and keep it in the fridge, the pancakes will be even fluffier!

Serves
4

HUEVOS RANCHEROS

A hearty, nutritious traditional Mexican breakfast that works beautifully in a wood oven. Fast and easy to prepare, it's a good one to make use of the oven if you are firing it up for lunch that day. I've eaten this dish a number of ways, the traditional way being with flash-fried corn tortillas as a base topped with fried eggs and a thick spicy salsa. Delicious. The less traditional but equally tasty way is to cook up a dish of sauce and cook the eggs directly in it. I prefer the latter. Plus it is better suited to wood ovens.

Ingredients

A splash of oil
½ white onion, chopped
1 garlic clove, crushed
2 tsp taco seasoning (see page 12)
1 tbsp tomato purée
2 x 400g cans chopped tomatoes or 1 litre passata
4 large free-range eggs
Small bunch of fresh coriander, chopped
Small handful of crumbled feta cheese
1 jalapeño chilli, finely sliced
8 tortillas, wrapped in foil and warmed in the oven for 5–10 minutes

Method

ROASTING – 160–200°C

Add the oil, onion and garlic to a frying pan and fry gently. Don't let the garlic brown or it will go bitter.

Stir in the taco seasoning and tomato purée and cook for a further 2 minutes.

Add the chopped tomatoes and cook for about 15 minutes, stirring every now and then.

Using the back of a dessert spoon, make four wells in the sauce and carefully crack an egg into each.

Slide back into the oven for another 4–5 minutes until the eggs are cooked but the yolks remain runny.

Sprinkle with the coriander, feta and chilli. Serve with the warmed tortillas.

> **Top tip** Once you have warmed the tortillas, keep them in the foil and wrap the whole lot in a tea towel or place inside a small cool box to keep nice and warm until you are ready to serve.

Serves 4

GALLO PINTO

I visited Costa Rica several years ago and spent every day surfing its bathwater-warm, crystal-clear, beautiful waves on a backdrop of incredible beaches, mountains and rainforest reaching the clouds. An incredible place. A day in the waves requires a hearty, nutritious breakfast that sustains you for the day, and luckily the Costa Ricans' favourite breakfast dish does just that. A mix of savoury, spiced rice with black beans, pepper and onion is typically served alongside a pile of scrambled or fried eggs, avocado, strong black coffee and, in my case, all the bacon.

Ingredients

2 tbsp olive oil
1 red pepper, finely diced
1 small yellow onion, finely diced
2 garlic cloves, minced
400g can cooked black beans, drained and rinsed
200ml vegetable stock
75ml Lizano salsa (see below), plus a little extra
750g cooked rice, preferably day-old and refrigerated
Bunch of fresh coriander, chopped
Tabasco sauce

Method

ROASTING - 160-200°C

Heat the olive oil in a large dish, then sauté the red pepper and onion until soft. Add the garlic and cook for a further minute.

Add the black beans, stock and Lizano salsa, stirring to combine.

Gently stir in the cooked rice and cook until heated through and most of the liquid has been absorbed.

Stir in the coriander. Splash on a few more slugs of Lizano salsa and finish with a few splashes of a hot pepper sauce, such as Tabasco.

Pura vida, as they say in Costa Rica!

Lizano salsa can be purchased online (www.hot-headz.com/lizano-salsa) from my friend Stuart, who imports all the best sauces from around the world, especially hot ones! You can substitute Worcestershire sauce if necessary.

> **Top tip** As with any 'fried' rice dish, this works best with yesterday's leftover rice as the refrigerated grains are easier to separate and tend to stay intact.

Serves 8

GRANOLA

A breakfast staple in our house, made all the better from a lick of wood smoke.

Ingredients

125g almonds
125g pecans
150g pumpkin seeds
175g sunflower seeds
250g rolled oats
3 tbsp coconut oil
3 tbsp runny honey
4 tbsp ground cinnamon
125g raisins
75g dried cranberries

Method

ROASTING - 160-200°C

Blitz the nuts in a food processor for 20–30 seconds until roughly chopped.

Tip into a large bowl and add the seeds and oats.

Melt the coconut oil and honey together in a small saucepan.

Stir in the cinnamon, then pour into the bowl with the dry ingredients, mixing thoroughly. Spread out evenly onto a baking tray.

Roast in the wood oven for 20 minutes, shaking and stirring regularly (you may need to do this in batches) until evenly toasted.

Allow to cool, mix in the raisins and cranberries, and store in a large airtight container.

Makes
1kg

MILLIONAIRE BACON

At the time of writing this book, millionaire bacon is all the rage. It's what the hip young things are ordering with their smashed avocado on toast in San Francisco. Millionaire bacon sounds cool, but it's little more than thick-cut bacon treated to some spice rubs and then candied. Nothing that can't be easily and deliciously replicated in your wood oven. And it won't be costing you $7 a slice either!

Ideally, you'll have a friendly local butcher who slices their own bacon. Ask for the slices to be about 3mm thick. If not, get hold of the thickest-cut, dry-cured bacon you can find.

Ingredients

12–16 slices of bacon
(3 slices of really thick or
4 slices of regular per
person)
1 tbsp freshly ground black
pepper mixed with 1 tbsp
ground coriander (or 2
tbsp Chinese five-spice
powder)
100g muscovado sugar

Method

ROASTING – 160-200°C

Line a baking sheet with parchment and lay the strips of bacon next to each other with no overlaps.

Mix the dry ingredients together in a bowl and sprinkle liberally over each slice of bacon.

Slide into a low oven for 45 minutes, turning often, until the sugar has caramelised.

Allow to cool before getting stuck in.

Serves
4

STUFFED PORTOBELLO MUSHROOMS

Ingredients

4 large portobello
   mushrooms
100g Parmesan cheese
200g cream cheese
Small handful fresh basil,
   chopped
Salt and freshly ground
   black pepper
100g breadcrumbs

Method

SIZZLING HOT - 220-300°C

Carefully slice off the mushroom stalks. Lay the mushrooms gill-side up in a roasting dish and slide into a medium wood oven for about 15 minutes until cooked through.

Meanwhile, mix the cheeses, basil, and salt and black pepper together in a bowl.

Remove the mushrooms from the oven and gently fill each one with the cheesy stuffing, then top with the breadcrumbs.

Return to the oven for a further 5–6 minutes until the breadcrumbs are crispy and golden.

Use this recipe as a base and get creative with it. You can add all sorts of interesting ingredients to the cream cheese to make different stuffings.

Here are some ideas:
Roasted and chopped red peppers
Crispy bacon bits
'Nduja
Wilted and chopped spinach
Garlic

Serves
2

PIZZAS

THE PIZZA COOKING PROCESS

Mankind has been making simple flatbreads and adding toppings since caveman times, but the first 'proper' pizza as we know it today is believed to have been made in Naples a few hundred years ago.

More recently, the Associazione Verace Pizza Napoletana, or True Neapolitan Pizza Association, was founded to set in place the ground rules as to what can be called an authentic Neapolitan pizza. Among others, the rules state that the pizza must be baked in a wood-fired domed oven, the base must be hand-kneaded and must not be rolled out with a rolling pin (you must use your hands to stretch it out), and the pizza must not exceed 35cm in diameter or be more than one-third of a centimetre thick at the centre. Unesco view this as such an important part of a unique cultural and gastronomic tradition that they awarded the art of 'Pizzaiuolo' world heritage status!

So there is your goal!

The perfect pizza oven is designed so that the heat rolls over the top of the pizza while the searing-hot floor seals the base instantly and cooks it through to a crisp, firm crust. Buying good ingredients and taking the time to allow the dough to do its thing will give you great sauces and great crusts.

The pizza-making process is simple and remains pretty much the same for all pizzas you'll be cooking.

GET READY

Have all your ingredients and tools laid out ready and your oven up to cruising altitude. You should be aiming for between 350–400°C to cook pizza.

Give your work surface a good covering of your dusting mix (see page 51) so that the dough does not stick.

**COOK ALL PIZZAS AT
SCREAMING HOT – 300–450°C**

STRETCH OUT THE DOUGH

It's actually quite hard to roll out a decent pizza with a rolling pin, so learn to do it properly with your hands instead. Rolling pins also knock all the air out of the dough, meaning your pizzas will not puff up well. Worse still, your card will be marked by the Associazione Verace Pizza Napoletana.

I was taught a very good tip in Puglia by a man who's been making pizza since before I was born:

STRETCH OUT THE EDGE OF THE PIZZA AND THE CENTRE WILL SORT ITSELF.

PLACE THE DOUGH BALL IN THE MIDDLE OF YOUR WORK SURFACE AND USE THE PALM OF YOUR HAND TO GENTLY SQUASH IT DOWN IN THE MIDDLE.

PICK UP THE DOUGH BY THE EDGE, HOLDING IT UP VERTICALLY, AND START TO TURN IT THROUGH YOUR HANDS AS THOUGH YOU WERE FEEDING A STEERING WHEEL THROUGH A BEND IN YOUR DRIVING TEST. MAKE SURE THE CENTRE OF THE PIZZA DOES NOT GET TOO THIN.

ONCE THE PIZZA IS THINNED OUT TO A HALF-DECENT SIZE, YOU CAN GIVE IT AN EXTRA STRETCH BY LAYING IT OVER THE BACKS OF YOUR KNUCKLES AND THEN GENTLY PULLING YOUR HANDS APART TO MAKE THE BASE LARGER. PRACTICE MAKES PERFECT, BUT IF YOU ARE FINDING THIS A BIT FIDDLY, LAY THE DOUGH BALL ON A WELL-DUSTED WORK SURFACE AND PUSH IT INTO A PIZZA SHAPE USING YOUR FINGERS.

LAY THE BASE ONTO A WOODEN PEEL THAT HAS BEEN WELL COVERED IN DUSTING MIX (SEE PAGE 51). AN IDEAL PIZZA SHAPE HAS A SLIGHTLY RAISED RIM TO HELP KEEP THE SAUCE AND TOPPINGS IN PLACE.

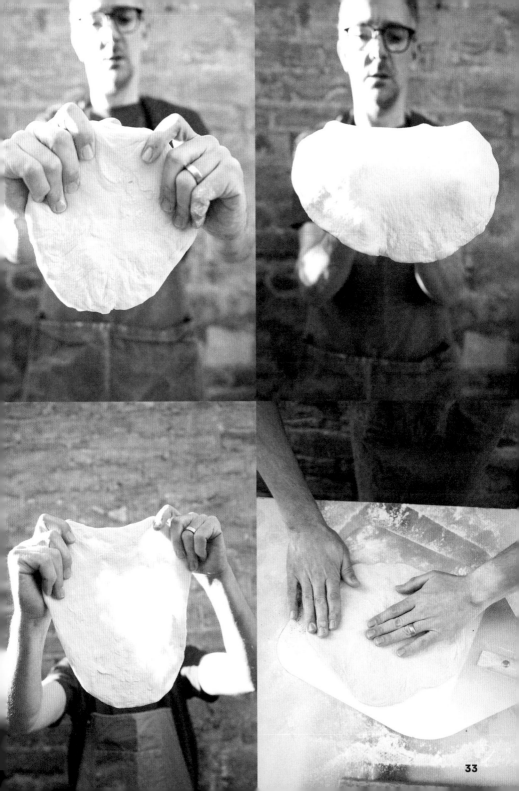

ADD THE TOPPINGS

Less is more when it comes to pizzas, especially when it comes to sauces.

Too much pomodoro will make your pizza soggy and will also make it harder to transfer to the oven.

Drop a few decent tablespoons of sauce in the centre of the base and use the back of the spoon in a spiral motion to evenly spread the sauce out to about 1cm from the edge.

Do the same with garlic purée, using only a couple of teaspoons worth, not tablespoons. Other toppings should be added according to your chosen recipe.

SLIDE THE PIZZA INTO THE OVEN

Keep your pizza peels clean and dry. Any spilt pomodoro sauce or cheese will cause the dough to stick and it won't easily slide into or out of the oven.

WATCH AND TURN

If your oven is good and hot, you'll need to turn your pizza every 20 seconds or so (on average, it takes 60–90 seconds to cook a pizza).

Turning is easy: slide a metal peel under the pizza and draw it out of the oven, spin it by 90 degrees on the peel, then slide it back in. This process should take no more than a few seconds once you get the hang of it. With larger ovens, you can use the wall next to the opening of the oven to spin the pizza on the peel.

If you are having trouble sliding the pizzas in and out of the oven, then get hold of a couple of pizza dishes like you see in the big pizzeria chains. Lay your stretched-out base onto the dusted dish and go from there. The bases won't puff up quite as well, but it will make life a lot easier.

Use your eye to see when the pizza is done. You want a firm, crispy base and the ingredients to be cooked, but not burnt, on top. If you have cheeses or pomodoro, then you want to see them bubbling.

A good test is to bring the pizza back out on the pizza peel and carefully lift up one side. If the base is cooked properly the whole pizza will lift as one, as though you were tipping up a plate; if it is still saggy, it needs to go back in.

If the base is still saggy but the top is burning, you may need to drag some of the coals back over the area you are cooking on and leave them there for 15–20 minutes before sweeping them back and resuming.

Too hot? If the base is burning before the toppings are cooked, then the floor is too hot and you need to cool it down. Use a damp cloth on the end of your pig flipper or similar and wipe it over the floor of the oven. This is also a good way to clean the oven, especially bits of burnt food mid-cooking.

SLICE AND EAT

Have a good-quality wooden chopping board within easy reach, along with a pizza slicer. Slide the pizza onto the board and drizzle with olive oil. Slice and transfer it to a serving platter or plate, leaving the board clean and ready for the next pizza.

> **Top tip** Once you have everything at the ready, it's always a good idea to run with a test pizza. If it works well, then the crowd will appreciate it; if not, you can bin it and nobody has lost their favourite pizza. A good test pizza is the garlic, herb and salt one (see page 59). It's cheap and easy to make, so no great loss if you find your oven is too hot or too cool, for example.

MANY HANDS MAKE LIGHT WORK

Making pizza is quick and easy on your own, but everyone loves to help out on pizza day, so put them to work!

THE DOUGH STRETCHER

This person is responsible for making sure the dough balls are brought out in a timely manner, stretching them out and getting them ready for the topper to get to work.

THE FIRE MONITOR

A great job for that friend who loves burning stuff! The main responsibilities here are regular oven temperature checks and the addition of logs as and when required. My friend George chooses to ignore the laser thermometer and just stick his hand in the oven to gauge the heat. The sooner his hand hurts, the hotter the fire.

THE TOPPER

There are two approaches here. Either have one person responsible for topping everyone's pizza for them – shout out your order and the topper will make it for you. Or set up an area where everyone can create their own pizza with the help and guidance of the topper when required.

THE COOK

This job is all about sliding the finished pizza into the oven, watching it, turning it and sliding it back out. One for someone that likes staring at fire all afternoon.

THE SLICER

The cook should transfer the pizza onto the chopping board, where the slicer slices it up and distributes it to the crowd. While they have very little to do with the actual pizza-making process, they tend to take all the glory for the good ones.

THE BEER BRINGER

With everyone so hard at work it's very important to have the beers brought to the team members on a regular basis. A critical role.

As with all well-oiled machines, getting a good crew together is a great way to cook for a big crowd. Ideally, as soon as one pizza comes out the oven, the next is ready to go in, meaning that you can quite easily knock out 30 pizzas per hour from just one small pizza oven.

PIZZA ESSENTIALS

You don't need a huge amount of equipment to make pizza, but a few choice bits will make the job all the more enjoyable, and will make you look like a pro!

A LARGE MIXING BOWL FOR MAKING STARTERS AND MIXING, THEN PROVING THE DOUGH.

LARGE TRAYS TO STORE AND PROVE SHAPED DOUGH BALLS. I USE LARGE BAKING TRAYS.

TEA TOWELS, OR SIMILAR, LARGE ENOUGH TO COVER THE TRAYS.

DIGITAL SCALES ACCURATE TO 1G.

FINE SEMOLINA TO MAKE THE DUSTING MIX.

00 FLOUR TO MAKE THE DOUGH.

A DOUGH SCRAPER FOR MOVING THE WET, STICKY DOUGH AROUND AND FOR DIVIDING UP DOUGH BALLS.

A PIZZA SLICER. A DECENT KNIFE WILL DO, BUT A PIZZA SLICER MAKES LIFE EASIER. THE TWO STYLES ARE THE ROLLER WHEEL AND THE LARGE CRESCENT ROCKER. BOTH WORK WELL.

PIZZA PEELS. A WOODEN ONE FOR MAKING THE PIZZA ON AND SLIDING THE UNCOOKED PIZZAS INTO THE OVEN AND A METAL ONE FOR SLIDING PIZZAS BACK OUT OF THE OVEN.

A PIZZA SPINNER IS NOT ESSENTIAL, BUT THIS SMALL-HEADED, CIRCULAR PIZZA PEEL MAKES THE MID-COOK TURNING EASIER.

BOWLS FOR INGREDIENTS. PIZZA NIGHT CAN GET PRETTY MESSY, SO ORGANISE ALL THE DIFFERENT TOPPINGS INTO LITTLE BOWLS FOR EASY ACCESS.

DOUGH

There are literally thousands of dough recipes and everyone has their favourites or their secret tricks. Here are my three favourite dough recipes. They won't let you down.

For the very best pizza bases, use Italian type 00 flour that is milled very fine for a silky-smooth and super-stretchy dough. If you can't find it, use a good strong white bread flour.

RECIPE 1 - QUICK PIZZA DOUGH
(READY TO COOK IN 2 HOURS)

This is a really easy pizza dough recipe given to me by master baker Tom Herbert many years ago.

Makes four 30cm pizzas

7g sachet dried yeast
300ml warm water
50ml olive oil
560g type 00 flour, plus extra for dusting
10g Maldon sea salt

Mix the dried yeast in a jug with the water and oil and wait 5–10 minutes until the mixture starts to bubble.

Add the flour and salt to a large bowl, then pour the liquid over.

Mix all the ingredients together, then tip out onto a floured board and knead for 15 minutes. Alternatively, use a food processor fitted with a dough hook on speed 1 for 10 minutes.

Once the dough is smooth, return it to the bowl, cover and leave it somewhere warm for about 1 hour until it has doubled in size. It is now ready to make into dough balls.

RECIPE 2 - OVERNIGHT PIZZA DOUGH
(READY TO COOK IN 24–48 HOURS)

Putting in some extra effort the day before pays off and it is well worthwhile if you are feeding a crowd. The overnight 'ferment' in this recipe gives the bases more flavour as well as a lovely chew.

Makes eight 30cm pizzas

DAY 1: MAKE THE SPONGE

500g type 00 flour
600ml warm water
2 x 7g sachets dried yeast

In a large mixing bowl, stir the flour, water and dried yeast into a thick batter-like consistency called a sponge, cover and leave overnight at room temperature.

DAY 2

500g type 00 flour, plus extra for dusting
20g Maldon sea salt

A few hours before you plan to cook, place the sponge and the remaining ingredients in a large mixing bowl, mix well, then knead for 15 minutes.

This is much easier to make with a food processor fitted with a dough hook, kneading for about 10 minutes.

Set the dough aside in a covered bowl for about 1 hour until doubled in size. It is now ready to make into dough balls.

RECIPE 3 - SOURDOUGH

Use the cast-iron-pot sourdough bread recipe (see page 187) as your base for this dough, but swap the malted bread flour for type 00 white flour. If you find the dough too wet, keep sprinkling additional small handfuls of flour over the mix and incorporate them. Although it is harder to handle, a wetter dough makes thinner, puffier pizza bases!

SHAPING THE DOUGH BALLS

Tip the dough onto a well-floured work surface and use a dough scraper to divide it into pieces. Each piece should weigh about 225g for a 30cm pizza. Size-wise, this is somewhere in between a snooker ball and a tennis ball.

Place your hand over the ball like you are doing 'spider fingers' and move over and over in a circular motion until the ball is smooth and round.

Place on a dusted tray, smoother and tauter side up, then cover with a tea towel for the final prove.

FREEZING THE DOUGH

Pizza dough freezes really well, so if you are investing the time in making an overnight batch, why not make double the quantity and freeze it.

The ideal point at which to freeze the dough is once you have divided it into balls but before you shape the balls and let them go through their final prove.

The best way to freeze them, if you have the space, is to lay the dough balls out on a plate or tray lined with baking paper and put the tray in the freezer. Once the balls have frozen, tip them into a zip-lock bag.

Next time you want pizza, grab as many dough balls as you need and allow them to defrost and prove as normal. Allow 2 hours for this.

Top tip Clean sticky dough off your hands by rubbing them with dry flour.

BASE INGREDIENTS

HOUSE POMODORO SAUCE

Learn to love this sauce and tweak it to make your own. It's going to be an integral part of most of the pizzas you make, so get it just right. Try swapping the oregano for basil, or adding some chilli flakes. If you have the time, make the sauce with fresh tomatoes using the method described below.

Makes enough for 8–10 pizzas

1L good-quality, Italian passata
2 garlic cloves, kept whole
1 tsp sugar
1 tsp dried oregano
1 tbsp red wine vinegar
Pinch of Maldon sea salt and freshly ground black pepper

Mix all the ingredients together in a pan and simmer gently for 5–10 minutes.

Fish out and discard the garlic and allow the sauce to cool.

This sauce freezes really well, so make a big batch and divide it up into your usual family-size portions.

UNCOOKED POMODORO SAUCE

A pomodoro sauce can be just as lovely made from uncooked tomatoes – it keeps the lovely colour and fresh tomato flavour.

1kg best ripe San Marzano tomatoes
Generous pinch of Maldon sea salt and freshly ground black pepper
Small handful of fresh basil, finely chopped

Using a sharp paring knife, score a small cross in the bottom of each tomato.

Bring a large pan of water to the boil, then carefully drop in the tomatoes and immediately remove from the heat.

After about 2 minutes, the tomato skins will start to peel off. Using a slotted spoon, transfer the tomatoes to a bowl of cold water.

Peel off and discard the tomato skins. Cut each skinned tomato in half, scooping out and discarding the seeds. Chop the tomatoes and add them to a bowl, crushing to a pulp with your hands.

Season well with the salt and black pepper, then stir in the basil. Chill in the fridge overnight and then allow to return to room temperature before using.

Confession: I have, on many an occasion, used a good-quality passata straight from the bottle with good results. It's a little thinner than a proper tomato sauce, so your pizzas might be a bit sloppy, but if you are short of time, go for it!

SIMPLE POMODORO SAUCE

Add a generous slug of olive oil to a heavy-based pan, then add 2–3 crushed garlic cloves, a small handful of fresh oregano leaves and 1 litre of passata (or 2 cans chopped tomatoes). Cook down for 20–25 minutes until the sauce is thick and the oil has started to separate from the tomatoes.

GARLIC PURÉE/CONFIT

8 bulbs of garlic
500ml olive oil
12 fresh thyme sprigs

Separate the garlic cloves and remove the skins. Add to a baking dish, submerge in the oil and add the thyme.

Bake in a medium oven for about 40 minutes until the cloves are tender.

They will keep (in the oil) in an airtight container for up to two months.

Whenever pizza day is approaching, or you need garlic purée for another dish, remove the cloves from the oil and smash in a mortar and pestle, or whizz in a food processor with a generous pinch of Maldon sea salt.

HERBS

I like to have fresh basil, fresh oregano and a little shaker filled with dried mixed Italian herbs on standby for every pizza day.

DUSTING MIX

Combine fine semolina with type 00 flour in equal parts and add to a shaker for easy use. An old jam jar with holes poked through the lid works well.

OLIVE OIL

A good-quality olive oil is essential in pizza making. Not only is it a fundamental ingredient in the dough, but it's also used for pre- or post- (or both) oven drizzling.

MOZZARELLA CHEESE

We're going to a lot of trouble to make great pizza, so don't spoil it with poor cheese.

HERE IS WHAT YOU NEED TO KNOW: THE BEST CHEESE FOR PIZZA IS FRESH COW'S MILK MOZZARELLA, ROUGHLY TORN INTO 2CM PIECES.

Take the drained mozzarella ball and tear it into several small marble-sized pieces. You will use approximately two balls for every three pizzas, but adjust the amount you use to personal preference as well as keeping it in balance with the other ingredients.

An ever-increasing and ever more baffling array of 'mozzarella' cheese is now available, from cow's milk to buffalo, packed in little bags filled with water, or sold in dry blocks or even pre-grated.

Generally speaking, true buffalo-milk mozzarella is stronger flavoured, more succulent and open textured than the equivalent cow's milk variety. However, it liquefies very easily, meaning it is much wetter to cook with. It sounds lovely and authentic to be using buffalo mozzarella on your pizza, but you are going to end up with soggy pizza – and nobody wants that – so save it for eating fresh on the side; it's delicious.

While any mozzarella made in Italy with buffalo milk can be called 'mozzarella di bufala', when you see 'Mozzarella di Bufala Campana', then you are looking at a DOC-status cheese that must be made from buffalo milk in the Campana region of Italy and you are in for a treat. But don't cook with it!

The vac-packed blocks of cheese are the opposite. They are dry, rubbery and do not give off enough moisture, never melting into that gooey pizza nirvana.

Steer clear at all costs of the pre-grated bags as the cheese is coated in cornflour to stop it sticking together. You'll find it a dry, bland product that will ruin your pizza.

PIZZA BIANCA WITH SAUSAGE, POTATO & ROSEMARY

Ingredients

1 pizza base, stretched and
   ready
Olive oil
100g sausage meat, in
   marble-size clumps
2 large Charlotte potatoes,
   peeled, cooked and sliced
   into 0.5cm rounds
Fresh rosemary, leaves
   stripped from the stalk

Method

Drizzle the pizza base with oil.

Dot with the sausage meat and potatoes, then sprinkle with
rosemary.

When cooked, drizzle with oil.

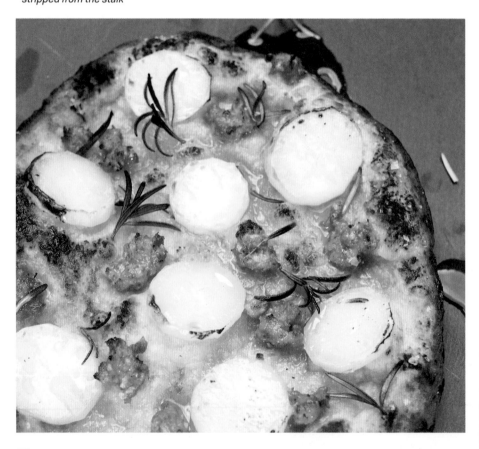

PIZZA BIANCA WITH ROAST KALE & FETA

Ingredients

*A few kale leaves, ribs
  removed*
Olive oil
*1 pizza base, stretched
  and ready*
*1–2 tsp garlic purée
  (see page 51)*
80g feta cheese

Method

Coarsely chop the kale leaves, toss in oil and slide into the oven on a baking tray for a few minutes until wilted.

Smear the garlic purée over the pizza base.

Dot with the feta and top with the kale.

When cooked, drizzle with oil.

PIZZA BIANCA – JEN & GEORGE'S PRAWN PIZZA

Ingredients

1 pizza base, stretched and
  ready
1–2 tsp garlic purée
  (see page 51)
Chilli flakes
Oregano
200g cooked king prawns
Maldon sea salt
Olive oil

Method

Smear the garlic purée over the pizza base.

Sprinkle with chilli flakes and oregano, then top with the prawns.

Season with salt.

When cooked, drizzle with oil.

PIZZA BIANCA WITH TURNIP TOPS & SAUSAGE

Turnip tops are an incredibly popular dish in Puglia, served mixed in with pasta, in bean purées or on top of pizzas. Delicious but easily substituted for other greens – you can, for example, swap them for wild garlic when the leaves appear in the early spring.

Ingredients

Handful of turnip tops,
  Swiss chard or beetroot
  tops
1 pizza base, stretched and
  ready
Olive oil
100g Italian sausage meat,
  in marble-size clumps
Maldon sea salt

Method

Blanch the leaves for a few minutes until tender, then drain and dry thoroughly.

Drizzle the pizza base with oil, then dot with the sausage meat and clumps of the wilted leaves. Season with salt.

When cooked, drizzle with oil.

PIZZA BIANCA, PROFUMO DI BOSCO

Ingredients

1 pizza base, stretched and
  ready
1–2 tsp garlic purée (see
  page 51)
Handful of mixed wild
  mushrooms
Handful of roasted ceps
  (see page 175)
Maldon sea salt
Small handful of rocket
Olive oil

Method

Smear the garlic purée over the pizza base.

Sprinkle with the wild mushrooms and roasted ceps.

Season with salt.

When cooked, sprinkle over the rocket and drizzle with oil.

PIZZA BIANCA WITH GARLIC, HERB & SALT

Ingredients

1 pizza base, stretched and
  ready
1–2 tsp garlic purée
  (see page 51)
Herbs of choice (fresh or
  dried are fine)
Maldon sea salt
Olive oil

Method

Smear the garlic purée over the pizza base.

Sprinkle with herbs and season with salt.

When cooked, drizzle with oil.

PIZZA BIANCA WITH MUSHROOM & ROSEMARY

Ingredients

1 pizza base, stretched and
  ready
1–2 tsp garlic purée
  (see page 51)
Fresh rosemary, leaves
  stripped from the stalk
Fresh thyme, leaves
  stripped from the stalk
Small handful of thinly
  sliced mushrooms (as thin
  as you can)
Maldon sea salt
Olive oil

Method

Smear the garlic purée over the pizza base.

Sprinkle with the herbs, then top with mushrooms.

Season with salt.

When cooked, drizzle with oil.

PIZZA BIANCA WITH RED CHICORY & GORGONZOLA

Ingredients

Handful of red chicory
  leaves
Olive oil
1 pizza base, stretched and
  ready
1–2 tsp garlic purée
  (see page 51)
80g Gorgonzola cheese
Mozzarella cheese, torn into
  chunks

Method

Smear the garlic purée over the pizza base.

Dot with the Gorgonzola and mozzarella.

When cooked, add the red chicory leaves and drizzle with oil.

PIZZA BIANCA WITH SPINACH & EGG

Ingredients

1 pizza base, stretched and
  ready
1–2 tsp garlic purée (see
  page 51)
Generous handful of
  spinach, washed and dried
Nutmeg
Small handful of Parmesan
  cheese, grated
2 eggs
Maldon sea salt
Olive oil

Method

Smear the garlic purée over the pizza base.

Add the spinach and grate over a little nutmeg.

Top with the Parmesan and carefully break the eggs into the centre of the pizza.

Season with salt.

When cooked, drizzle with oil.

PIZZA BIANCA WITH ANCHOVY & CAPERS

Umami packed!

Ingredients

1 pizza base, stretched and
　ready
1-2 tsp garlic purée
　(see page 51)
6-8 anchovy fillets
Mozzarella cheese, torn into
　chunks
1 tbsp capers, drained
Sprinkling of oregano
1 tsp chilli flakes
Olive oil

Method

Smear the garlic purée over the pizza base.

Dot with the anchovies and mozzarella.

Sprinkle over the capers, oregano and chilli flakes.

When cooked, drizzle with oil.

PIZZA MARINARA

This is believed to be the oldest of all pizzas and along with the margherita, is considered by purists as being one of the only two authentic pizzas. It is called 'marinara' because it was traditionally prepared by 'la marinara', the seaman's wife, for her seafaring husband after he returned from fishing trips in the Bay of Naples.

Ingredients

1 pizza base, stretched and ready
1–2 tsp garlic purée (see page 51)
2–3 tbsp pomodoro sauce (see page 48)
Fresh oregano leaves
Maldon sea salt
Olive oil

Method

Smear the garlic purée over the pizza base.

Spread the pomodoro sauce on top and sprinkle with oregano.

Season with salt.

When cooked, drizzle with oil.

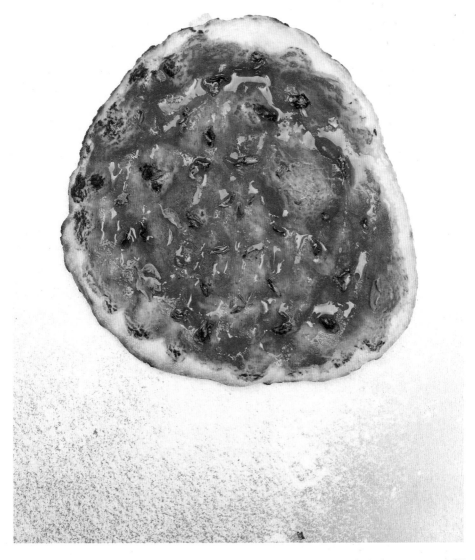

CLASSIC MARGHERITA

A good margherita takes some beating in my book.

Ingredients

1 pizza base, stretched and
  ready
1–2 tsp garlic purée
  (see page 51)
2–3 tbsp pomodoro sauce
  (see page 48)
Mozzarella cheese, torn into
  chunks
Fresh basil leaves
Olive oil

Method

Smear the garlic purée over the pizza base.

Spread the pomodoro sauce on top and dot on the mozzarella.

Sprinkle with basil leaves.

When cooked, drizzle with oil.

PIZZA PUTTANESCA

Ingredients

1 pizza base, stretched and
   ready
1–2 tsp garlic purée
   (see page 51)
2–3 tbsp pomodoro sauce
   (see page 48)
Small handful of anchovy
   fillets
Small handful of capers,
   drained
Small handful of mixed
   green and black olives
Fresh chilli to taste
Mozzarella cheese, torn into
   chunks
Olive oil

Method

Smear the garlic purée over the pizza base.

Spread the pomodoro sauce on top and dot on the anchovies.

Sprinkle with the capers, olives and chilli.

Dot the mozzarella on top.

When cooked, drizzle with oil.

PIZZA WITH PROSCIUTTO & ROCKET

Ingredients

1 pizza base, stretched and
ready
2–3 tbsp pomodoro sauce
(see page 48)
3–4 slices prosciutto ham,
torn into strips
Mozzarella cheese, torn into
chunks
Fresh oregano leaves
Handful of rocket
Olive oil

Method

Spread the pomodoro sauce over the pizza base.

Lay over the ham and dot on the mozzarella.

Sprinkle with oregano leaves.

When cooked, top with the rocket and drizzle with olive oil.

PIZZA WITH SALSICCIA & FENNEL SEED

Ingredients

100g Italian sausage meat
2 tsp fennel seeds
1 pizza base, stretched and
  ready
2–3 tbsp pomodoro sauce
  (see page 48)
Mozzarella cheese, torn into
  chunks
Olive oil

Method

Squeeze the sausage meat out of the skins into a bowl and mix in the fennel seeds.

Spread the pomodoro sauce over the pizza base.

Dot on the sausage meat and mozzarella.

When cooked, drizzle with oil.

PIZZA DIAVOLO

Ingredients

1 pizza base, stretched and
ready
2–3 tbsp pomodoro sauce
(see page 48)
Spicy salami, sliced
Fresh chilli, to taste
Small handful of capers,
drained
Mozzarella cheese, torn into
chunks
Chilli oil

Method

Spread the pomodoro sauce over the pizza base.

Lay over the salami and sprinkle over plenty of chilli and the capers.

Dot on the mozzarella.

When cooked, drizzle with chilli oil.

PIZZA WITH VODKA

According to my sister-in-law Brett, a native New Yorker, there is a pizza joint in Manhattan called Rubirosa, where people queue round the block for their famous vodka pizza.

This recipe, which is enough for 12–15 pizzas, is based on a classic American-Italian dish called 'penne alla vodka', a cream- and tomato-based sauce with a slug of vodka. The alcohol cooks off, leaving a hint of heat and a bite that cuts through the richness of the sauce.

Ingredients

Generous glug of olive oil,
   plus extra for drizzling
4 garlic cloves, crushed
1 tsp dried oregano
2 x 400g cans Italian
   chopped tomatoes
200ml double cream
80ml vodka
Maldon sea salt and freshly
   ground black pepper
12–15 pizza bases, stretched
   and ready
500g mozzarella cheese,
   torn into 3cm chunks
Handful of fresh basil leaves

Method

Heat the oil in a skillet. Add the garlic and sauté until soft, but don't let it colour. Add the oregano, then tip in the tomatoes.

Return to the oven to cook down for about 20 minutes, stirring often. Add the cream and cook for a further 15 minutes. Then add the vodka and cook for 10 minutes more. Season with salt and black pepper. When cool, blitz in a blender until smooth.

To make up the pizzas, spread 2–3 tablespoons of sauce over each pizza base. Add 8–10 mozzarella pieces per pizza and a sprinkling of basil leaves. Drizzle with oil and cook.

For guests with a sore head from the night before, turn this vodka pizza into a Bloody Mary pizza by adding freshly sliced red chilli, a light sprinkling of celery salt and a handful of plump green olives.

PIZZA FUMÉE

The smokiness of traditional Italian scamorza cheese really complements the wood-fired flavours.

Ingredients

1 pizza base, stretched and
  ready
2–3 tbsp pomodoro sauce
  (see page 48)
Few slices of speck, roughly
  torn
100g smoked scamorza
  cheese
Mozzarella cheese, torn into
  chunks
Olive oil

Method

Spread the pomodoro sauce over the pizza base.

Dot on the speck, scamorza and mozzarella.

When cooked, drizzle with oil.

PIZZA WITH FETA & ROCKET

Ingredients

1 pizza base, stretched and
  ready
1–2 tsp garlic purée
  (see page 51)
Few sprigs of fresh oregano
  and rosemary
75g feta cheese, crumbled
Small handful of rocket
Olive oil

Method

Smear the garlic purée over the pizza base.

Sprinkle with the oregano and rosemary.

When cooked, sprinkle over the feta and rocket, then drizzle with oil.

PIZZETTE

Mini pizzas are great for passing round and nibbling on with drinks before the main event. They are easy to hold and eat with one hand, without the need for plates. You can roll them all out individually from small dough balls, but it's easier to roll out a bigger ball of dough and use a 6cm cookie cutter to make little discs. Once made, set the discs aside for 20 minutes to rise.

Top and cook as with regular pizzas – just smaller!

CALZONE

Calzone, to me, is where worlds collide. They are the Cornish pasty of the pizza world. The method for making them remains the same, regardless of your choice of filling. The trick is not to overstuff them as this may cause them to burst during cooking.

Method

SIZZLING HOT - 220-300°C

Start off with a regular-size pizza base (about 30cm in diameter). Add your chosen ingredients to one half of the base, leaving a 1.5cm border around the edge. Carefully fold over the base, squeezing out as much air as you can.

The edges should stick together, but dampen them with a little water if they've dried out too much. Press down around the edges to seal; you can use the tines of a fork to make it look fancy, if you like.

Cook for 6–8 minutes in a slightly cooler oven than a traditional pizza (about 220°C), rotating halfway through cooking. When cooked, allow to rest for a few minutes before slicing open.

Filling suggestions

Sautéed spinach, ricotta, grated Parmesan, mozzarella and nutmeg

Shredded chicken, mozzarella and pomodoro sauce

Pepperoni, mushroom and ricotta

Oven-roasted broccoli and blue cheese

Chicken, bacon and Cheddar

Oven-roasted meat ragu with mozzarella and Parmesan

Roast butternut, sage and ricotta

Or veer away from the traditional and opt for one of these suggestions:

Tandoori chicken

Beef barbacoa and goat's cheese

Philly cheese-steak (thinly sliced cooked steak, oven-roasted red peppers, spring onions and Cheddar or similar cheese)

Avocado, chicken and bacon

Romanesco cauliflower cheese

Scrambled eggs, bacon and fried potatoes

Prawns, chilli, garlic and parsley

Club calzone (sliced ham, turkey and Emmental with mayo and sliced tomatoes)

Leftover lamb hotpot with pickled beetroot or pickled cabbage

You can even go radical and turn calzone into desserts. How about peanut butter and chocolate buttons, or smashed bananas and caramel sauce?

FROM THE SEA

FISH EN PAPILLOTE

This is a great dish to prepare a few hours ahead of time and throw in the oven at the last minute. It is a very delicate and tasty way to cook white fish that locks in all the juices and flavour. So succulent and flavoursome.

Ingredients

1 leek
1 carrot
1 fennel bulb
Butter, for greasing
4 chunky white fish fillets, such as cod, haddock or pollack
Maldon sea salt and freshly ground black pepper
Small handful of dill (fresh or dried)
1 lemon, thinly sliced

TO SERVE
Boiled new potatoes
Creamed spinach

Method

ROASTING – 160–200°C

Shred all the vegetables very finely. A mandolin makes light work of this, but mind your fingers!

Tear off a piece of foil about 45cm long. If your foil is thin, then double it up.

Spread a generous layer of butter in the middle of the foil, a little larger than the fish fillet.

Place a small handful of shredded vegetables over the butter, then lay a fish fillet on top.

Season with salt and black pepper and a sprinkling of dill. Add a couple of lemon slices on top and then add a second handful of shredded vegetables. Fold the foil parcel up, removing any air as you go.

Repeat for the remaining three fillets, then slide into the oven for 15–20 minutes.

Serve with buttered boiled new potatoes and creamed spinach.

A note on foil I'm a real foil snob. I cannot bear the wafer-thin bog-standard stuff most supermarkets peddle. It pierces and rips too easily, ruining dishes and causing you to use three times as much. The best bet is to hunt out some catering-grade thick foil. Not only is it robust enough to do the job, but it tends to come in wider rolls, making it much easier to cover baking trays and the like. My personal preference is Costco's own brand. It's been my go-to foil for about eight years now. Yes, I am a foil geek. Sad isn't it?

> **Top tip** This is a very versatile way to cook fish – you can adapt this recipe to use your favourite flavours. Try using sliced chillies, lemongrass, ginger and lime zest, or adding a few drops of white wine. Or tomato and oregano with a little olive oil.

Serves
4

WHOLE BAKED SEA BREAM

Roasting a whole fish is a wonderful thing to do in a wood oven. You get all that delicious wood-fire seared flavour without the hassle of trying to flip it over like you do with a barbecue! Use the method described here for any medium-size whole fish.

Ingredients

Method

ROASTING - 160-200°C

*1 sea bream, gutted,
  descaled and cleaned*
*Maldon sea salt and freshly
  ground black pepper*
*Bunch of fresh tarragon
  (or your herb of choice),
  chopped*
1 lemon, sliced into wedges
Olive oil

Make 3–4 diagonal slashes down both sides of the fish, then brush inside and out with a thin coating of oil and season generously with salt and black pepper.

Stuff the cavity with the tarragon and as many lemon wedges as will fit.

Place into a hot oiled skillet and slide into the oven for 10–12 minutes until cooked through.

Serves
2

KING PRAWNS WITH GARLIC, BUTTER & CHILLI

This is a staple dish of pretty much every coastal Mediterranean restaurant where freshness of ingredients sings through. I could happily eat it for lunch every day of the year, sitting by the sea in the sunshine, sipping on a cold glass of vino. I like to cook this in small, shallow earthenware dishes straight from the oven to the table, with the prawns still sizzling. Get the biggest prawns you can: 7–10cm-long whopper tiger prawns look and taste fantastic.

Ingredients

6 large raw tiger prawns in their shells (or 12 regular king prawns)

25g butter

2 tbsp olive oil

3 garlic cloves, thinly sliced

1 red chilli, thinly sliced

Juice of ½ lemon

1 tbsp parsley, finely chopped, to garnish

Maldon sea salt

Method

SIZZLING HOT - 220-300°C

Rinse the prawns then pat dry with kitchen roll.

Heat a skillet in the wood oven, then add the butter, oil, garlic and chilli. Cook for a few minutes, then add the prawns, stirring so that they are evenly coated in the buttery oil.

Cook the prawns for 3–4 minutes until they turn pink and start to char a little.

Remove the pan from the heat, squeeze over the lemon juice and garnish with the parsley.

Season with salt and serve piping hot.

> **Top tip** Eating prawns is a messy business! Put a finger bowl with a few slices of lemon on the table for each person to rinse their fingers in.

Serves 2

SCALLOPS

Scallops are wonderful cooked in a wood oven. They're excellent seared hot and fast, building a little char on the outside but remaining tender, juicy and sweet inside. They really seem to take on the flavour of the wood fire well, but best of all they come ready in their own little cooking dishes! They can be cooked all sorts of different ways, but here are two of my favourites.

SCALLOPS WITH 'NDUJA BUTTER

'Nduja is a fiery, bright red, spreadable salami from Calabria that packs a powerful flavour punch.

Ingredients

Method

SIZZLING HOT - 220-300°C

100g 'nduja
50g butter
6 scallop shells
18 scallops, coral removed
Small handful of fresh
  parsley, finely chopped

Serves 3

Bring the 'nduja and butter to room temperature, then mash together.

Rinse and dry the scallop shells. Add three scallops to each shell and top with 1 tablespoon of the 'nduja butter per shell, evenly spread over the scallops.

Lay the shells on a baking tray and slide into the oven for a few minutes until the scallops are cooked through and starting to caramelise on top. When cooked, sprinkle the top with the parsley.

...OR SAUTÉED IN A FRYING PAN WITH BUTTER, LEMON & HERBS

Ingredients

Method

50g butter
Splash of olive oil
18 scallops, coral removed
Juice of 1 lemon
Small handful of fresh
  oregano and parsley

Serves 3

Heat the butter and oil in a frying pan until bubbling hot. Gently lay down the scallops and shake them around in the pan so that they are coated all over in the buttery juices.

Slide the pan into the oven for a few minutes until the scallops are cooked through and starting to caramelise on top – there's no need to flip them over as the oven will sear the top as they cook.

When cooked, remove from the oven, squeeze over the lemon juice and sprinkle with the herbs.

PRAWN KUSHIYAKI SKEWERS

Ingredients

2 tsp clear honey

Juice of 1 lime, plus 1 lime,
cut into wedges, to serve

1 tsp grated ginger

2 tsp sweet chilli sauce, plus
extra to serve

1 tsp chilli flakes

12 king prawns, shelled and
cleaned

Small handful of
fresh coriander, chopped

Method

SIZZLING HOT - 220-300°C

In a small bowl, make a sauce by mixing together the honey, lime juice, ginger, sweet chilli sauce and chilli flakes.

Place the raw prawns and the sauce into a small freezer bag, squeeze the air out and seal, then refrigerate for 2 hours.

You will need six small bamboo skewers. Thread two prawns onto each skewer.

Heat a cast-iron griddle in the oven until hot, then place the prawns down and slide back into the oven. Cook for 1–2 minutes until the prawns are pink, plump and delicious. There's no need to turn the prawns as the tops will sear in the oven.

Serve with a little more sweet chilli sauce as a dip alongside lime wedges and a sprinkling of coriander.

Serves
4

MONKFISH & CHORIZO SKEWERS

Monkfish is superb cooked over an open fire, whichever way you choose to prepare it. It holds up to strong flavours well, so you can use heavy rubs or powerful seasonings with it, and it is meaty enough to sear at a high temperature to develop a lovely crust. Monkfish tails are great roasted whole, but these skewers mean everything is in lovely bite-size pieces! A classic partner for monkfish is chorizo; the spicy, paprika flavour from the chorizo matches the monkfish superbly. This recipe also includes red onions and cherry tomatoes, giving sweet, spicy and juicy flavour-packed skewers.

Ingredients

4 large monkfish tails (ask your fishmonger to fillet them), cut into bite-size pieces

200g cooking chorizo, cut into 5mm thick slices

1 red onion, cut into 8 segments

30 cherry tomatoes halved

Good-quality olive oil

Salt and freshly ground black pepper

Juice of 1 lemon

Small handful of fresh parsley, chopped

Method

SIZZLING HOT – 220–300°C

Soak four wooden skewers in water for about 30 minutes to help prevent the ends from burning in the wood oven.

Thread the monkfish onto the skewers, alternating each chunk with a slice of chorizo, a piece of red onion and a tomato.

Drizzle the skewers with oil and season generously with salt and freshly ground black pepper.

Lay the skewers in a dish and slide into a medium oven for about 10 minutes until the fish starts to char, the onions soften and the cherry tomatoes blister and shrink down.

Squeeze over the lemon juice and once plated, sprinkle over the parsley.

Serve with Charlotte potatoes cut into small chunks and roasted in the oven with rosemary, garlic and red onion.

Serves
4

PAELLA

A true paella should be cooked outdoors, so you are halfway there by cooking this in your wood oven. A small 30cm paella pan will fit in most pizza ovens and can be used for all manner of dishes. It is well worth investing in one or two. Paella originates in the rice fields of the coastal city of Valencia on Spain's east coast. They throw in whatever is readily available, and so anything goes – rabbit, chicken, pork, frogs, shellfish, hunks of meaty fish and even whole small fish are all fair game. Go with what you fancy.

Ingredients

4–5 tbsp olive oil

1 large onion, finely chopped

1 red pepper, sliced

1 semi-cured chorizo (about 150g), sliced

2 garlic cloves, crushed

200g chopped tomatoes

Generous pinch of salt

½ tsp sugar

1 tsp sweet paprika

1 tsp turmeric

Good pinch of saffron threads

4 chicken thighs

400g Spanish paella rice

250ml white wine

750ml chicken stock, plus extra if needed

1 squid, cleaned and diced

16 mussels, scrubbed and cleaned

16 raw shell-on king prawns

Lemon wedges, to serve

Method

ROASTING – 160-200°C

Heat the paella pan in the oven for a few minutes with the olive oil.

Add the onion, red pepper, chorizo and garlic, sauté for a few minutes, then add the tomatoes.

Stir in the salt, sugar, paprika, turmeric and saffron. Add the chicken thighs and cook for a further few minutes until lightly browned.

Stir in the rice, then splash in the wine and stock. Stir again and spread everything out evenly in the pan, then cover and cook over a low heat for 20 minutes. If the rice looks too dry, you can add another splash of stock.

After 10–15 minutes, stir in the squid and place the mussels on top.

Add the king prawns after 5 minutes. Cover with foil and leave the seafood to cook for a further 5 minutes. Serve up straight from the dish with lemon wedges on the side.

A note on Socarrat *Socarrat is a lovely word the Spanish have for the crust of crunchy, chewy, browned rice that forms at the bottom of the paella pan. It's deeply flavoured and slightly sweet from the Maillard reaction, like the bark on the outside of a piece of roast beef. Socarrat, from the Spanish verb socarrar (to singe), is an intrinsic part of paella and is fought over in Spanish families because it is so damned delicious. Be very careful though, there is a very fine line between a beautifully chewy, toasted-brown crust, and bitter, burnt, black carbon.*

Serves 4

TERIYAKI & SESAME-SEED SALMON

Ingredients

4 salmon fillets
8 tbsp teriyaki sauce
1 tbsp vegetable oil
2 tbsp clear honey
3 tbsp sesame seeds

FOR THE SLAW

½ small red cabbage
½ small white cabbage
1 medium carrot
2 tbsp sesame seeds
   (toasted in a dry pan until
   golden brown)
1 fresh chilli, finely sliced
Handful of fresh coriander,
   chopped
Juice of 1 lime

Method

ROASTING - 160-200°C

Start by making the slaw. Using a mandolin on the finest setting, shred the red and white cabbages into a big bowl.

Grate in the carrot, then add the sesame seeds, chilli and coriander. Squeeze in the lime juice and mix to combine. Cover and refrigerate until ready to serve.

For the fish, put the salmon fillets and teriyaki sauce in a zip-lock bag, squeeze out the air and refrigerate for up to 4 hours.

Heat a skillet or roasting dish in the oven, then add the oil. Remove the fish from the bag and lay each fillet in the pan, skin-side down.

Slide back into the oven and cook for 5–7 minutes.

Drizzle with the honey and sprinkle with the sesame seeds. Slide back into the oven and cook for a further 5 minutes.

Serve the salmon with the slaw on the side.

Serves
4

SKATE WING

Ingredients

2 fresh skate wings
(weighing about 200g
each)
Maldon sea salt and freshly
ground black pepper
2 tbsp plain flour
100g butter
Juice of 1 small lemon
2 tbsp nonpareille capers,
rinsed
2 tbsp fresh flat-leaf parsley,
chopped

Method

ROASTING - 160-200°C

Slide a roasting dish into a medium oven to heat up.

Rinse the skate wings and pat dry with kitchen paper. Season both sides of the wings with salt and black pepper, then dust lightly with the flour.

Add one-third of the butter to the dish and gently lay down the skate wings. Slide back into the oven for 5 minutes, then gently turn over and cook for a further 5 minutes until the flesh firms up and the skin is golden.

Transfer the fish to warm serving plates and tent loosely with foil to keep warm while you work on the sauce.

Return the dish to the oven to heat up, then add the remaining butter and cook until it turns a caramel-brown colour and smells nutty, but be careful not to let it burn.

Remove the dish from the heat and stir in the lemon juice, capers and parsley. Pour the butter over the skate and serve immediately.

To jazz this dish up ever so slightly more, try adding 50g of cooked brown shrimp along with the capers.

Serves
2

PLANKED SALMON

Cooking the fish on a wooden plank is a terrific way to keep it moist, but it also adds great aroma and flavour.

Ingredients

2 salmon fillets

Small plank of oak, beech or other aromatic hard/ fruit wood, soaked for 2 hours

Maldon sea salt and freshly ground black pepper

1 lemon, thinly sliced

Bunch of fresh dill, chopped

Method

 SIZZLING HOT - 220-300°C

Lay the fish on the plank and season well with salt and black pepper. Lay a few slices of lemon over the top of each fillet and sprinkle with dill.

Slide into the oven for about 20 minutes until cooked through.

Feel free to mix up the seasonings (see below) here – salmon is great at standing up to big flavours!

Piri piri seasoning	Cajun rub
1½ tsp paprika	2 tsp salt
1 tsp dried oregano, crushed	2 tsp garlic powder
1 tsp ground ginger	2½ tsp paprika
1 tsp ground cardamom	1 tsp ground black pepper
1 tsp garlic powder	1 tsp onion powder
1 tsp onion powder	1 tsp cayenne pepper
½ tsp salt	1¼ tsp dried oregano
½ tsp ground piri piri or cayenne pepper	1¼ tsp dried thyme
	½ tsp red pepper flakes

Mix all the ingredients together in a bowl.

Transfer the rub to an airtight container – it will keep for up to 1 month.

Salmon works well with Chinese or Indian spices too.

Serves 2

OCTOPUS & MEXICAN BLACK BEANS

Ingredients

FOR THE OCTOPUS
Olive oil
Salt and freshly ground
   black pepper
Juice of 2 limes
450–500g baby octopus or
   tentacles, cleaned

FOR THE BLACK BEANS
30g butter
½ red onion, finely chopped
1 tsp cumin
3 garlic cloves, crushed
400g can black beans
100g cherry tomatoes,
   chopped
1 tbsp Tabasco/hot sauce
50ml vegetable stock
Chopped fresh coriander, to
   garnish

Method

SIZZLING HOT - 220-300°C

Start with the octopus. In a frying pan, add a decent splash of olive oil, a pinch of salt and a grinding of black pepper, along with the lime juice. Heat the pan until it gets nice and hot.

Add the octopus and cook for about 3 minutes each side, or until it colours nicely. Set aside.

For the black beans, heat the butter, onion, cumin and garlic in a separate frying pan until softened. Add the black beans, tomatoes, hot sauce and vegetable stock. Mix together and simmer on a medium heat for about 15 minutes, stirring all the time. The beans are done when the sauce has thickened.

Add the octopus and coriander and stir lightly.

Serve on soft warm tortillas, topped with more tomatoes, onion and coriander.

To serve
Soft warm tortillas
Finely chopped cherry tomatoes
Finely chopped onion
Chopped fresh coriander

Serves
2

BAKED SARDINES

Ingredients

2 red peppers (see note below)

3 tbsp olive oil, plus extra for drizzling

2 tbsp garlic purée (see page 51)

1 tbsp sugar

1 tsp red wine vinegar

350ml pomodoro sauce (see page 48)

8 fresh sardines, gutted and rinsed

Maldon sea salt and freshly ground black pepper

Handful fresh parsley, finely chopped

Crusty bread, to serve

Method

 ROASTING - 160-200°C

Roast the red peppers in a hot oven until charred all over.

Place them in a bowl and cover with clingfilm so that they steam.

When cool enough to handle, remove the blackened skin with kitchen paper. Slice open and remove the seeds and stalks, then slice into 5mm strips, drizzle with oil and set aside.

Add the oil and garlic purée to a skillet and slide into the oven to cook for 1–2 minutes.

Add the peppers, sugar, vinegar and pomodoro sauce. Stir well, bring to a simmer and cook down for 10 minutes.

Season the sardines with salt, black pepper and a drizzle of oil, then lay them onto the sauce in the skillet so that the sauce half covers them.

Slide back into the oven for a further 10 minutes until the fish is cooked through. Sprinkle with the parsley and serve with hunks of bread to mop up the juices.

> **Top tip** It's great to make more of these peppers than you need. Roast 5 or 6 red peppers, slice them and store in a jar of olive oil. They'll happily keep in the fridge for a week or two. Add them to pasta dishes or salads, use them to top omelettes or pizzas or pile them up on a piece of sourdough toast for a quick and tasty snack.

Serves 4

MAINS

WOOD-FIRED STEAK

I've always preferred a steak cooked in a flat-bottomed cast-iron skillet to one cooked on the grill bars of a barbecue. I think you get a much better and more even sear. The steak retains more moisture, you have more control over the cooking and it's easy to add an extra hit of flavour with some butter and herbs in the pan. Having said that, NOTHING quite beats the flavour of great steak hit with some live fire. Wood ovens present the best of both words: all the flavour and char of a fire, but the superior sear and moisture retention of cooking in a skillet. Make sure you use a thick, flat cast-iron pan, *not* a ridged one.

Ingredients

2 thick-cut (about 3cm
   thick) T-bone, sirloin or
   rib-eye steaks
Olive oil
Maldon sea salt and freshly
   ground black pepper
Large knob of butter
2–3 sprigs of fresh rosemary
3 garlic cloves, left whole
   and unpeeled

Method

SIZZLING HOT – 220-300°C

Place a cast-iron skillet in a medium oven until it is screaming hot.

Lightly oil the steaks and season generously with salt and black pepper.

Gently lay the steaks down into the pan and slide back into the oven. Flip after 2–3 minutes, then add the butter to the pan along with the rosemary and garlic.

Cook for a few more minutes, basting the meat with a spoon as you go. Continue to baste and flip until you reach your desired doneness (see the meat chart on page 13).

Remove steaks from the pan onto a plate, tip over the juices from the pan and rest under tented foil for ten minutes'

Slice onto a serving plate and pour over all the resting juices.

Serves
2

LAMB SHOULDER

I like to serve this with a simple mint sauce to cut through the rich meat.

Ingredients

2 carrots, roughly chopped

2 celery sticks, roughly
  chopped

1 onion, roughly chopped

3 ripe tomatoes, chopped

A few sprigs of fresh thyme
  and rosemary

10 cloves garlic, left whole

1 whole shoulder of lamb on
  the bone (weighing about
  2kg)

Maldon sea salt and freshly
  ground black pepper

250ml white wine

300ml lamb or chicken
  stock

FOR THE MINT SAUCE

1 bunch of fresh mint, stalks
  discarded

1 tbsp caster sugar

2 tbsp cider vinegar

Method

LOW AND SLOW - 120–160°C

Aim for a medium–low oven (140–150°C).

Put all the vegetables and herbs into a baking dish along with the garlic.

Season the lamb generously with salt and black pepper and lay it on top of the vegetables.

Pour in the wine and stock. Loosely cover with foil and roast for 3–4 hours.

The meat is done when it starts to fall off the bone and the strands can be pulled apart easily with the back of a spoon.

For the mint sauce, you can either chop up the mint super-fine by hand and mix in the other ingredients, or whack the lot in a blender and blitz. A mortar and pestle will do a good job too. The trick is to ensure you make the sauce a few hours in advance.

Serves
6-8

LASAGNE

This is quite a lengthy recipe that calls for a real slow-cook meat ragu to be made, then used in a lasagne. That means this dish gets two rides through the oven! Trust me – it is well worth the effort.

Ingredients

1 batch wood-fired ragu (see page 122)
1 pack (375g) dried lasagne sheets
100g freshly grated Parmesan cheese

FOR THE BÉCHAMEL SAUCE
80g butter
80g plain flour
1 litre
Pinch of freshly ground nutmeg

Method

ROASTING - 160-200°C

Start by making the béchamel sauce. Heat a saucepan in the oven, then melt the butter and stir in the flour until it makes a paste and reaches a cookie-dough colour and consistency. Add one-third of the milk and stir or whisk well until combined and lump-free. Add another one-third of the milk and repeat. Finally, add the remaining third of the milk and keep whisking until the sauce starts to simmer. Stir in the nutmeg.

To build the lasagne, spread a thin layer of ragu in the bottom of a 30cm square dish. Pour over a thin layer of béchamel sauce, then cover with lasagne sheets.

Repeat until you have almost reached the top of the dish. The final layers should be: ragu, lasagne sheets, béchamel, final lasagne sheets and a final layer of béchamel. So, remember to keep enough back for the final topping!

Sprinkle with the Parmesan, then slide into a medium oven for about 45 minutes until the top is brown and crispy and you can easily slide a sharp knife through the lasagne sheets. Allow to stand for 5–10 minutes before serving.

If you can, construct the lasagne a few hours (or even a day) before you plan to cook it. I'm not sure why, but it always seems to hold together better through cooking and will have a better texture that way.

Serves
8

ROAST ONION FRITTATA

Although they're at their very best while hot, this is a great one to bang in the oven after you've finished cooking for the day. Cook it now and have it cold for brunch or on a sandwich the next day. Yummy.

Whole books could be written just about frittata – there are so many iterations. It's really a blank canvas for you to work with. By all means, cook something well-considered, but equally delicious can be those 'ready, steady, cook' moments where you forage the fridge and go for it. Make sure any ingredients you are adding don't need much cooking time. So, if you are using peppers, then maybe roast them for a few minutes, or parboil potatoes until almost cooked through.

Ingredients

3 onions, left whole and unpeeled
10 large free-range eggs (I aim for 1½–2 eggs per person)
Maldon sea salt and freshly ground black pepper
Knob of butter

Method

ROASTING – 160–200°C

Put the onions in a roasting tray in the hot part of the oven and roast for about 1 hour, turning them every 15 minutes. Remove from the oven and allow to cool down enough to handle. Discard the charred outer layers, then slice up the lovely soft, smoky cooked insides.

The following goes for all frittatas! Add the eggs to a large bowl, season with salt and black pepper and beat well. Add the remaining ingredients and combine.

Rub the butter around the dish the onions were cooked in with some kitchen paper. Tip in the eggy mixture and, if you need to, poke the ingredients around a little bit to distribute them evenly.

Slide the dish into the oven and bake for about 15 minutes until the eggs have set firmly. Tip onto a chopping board and slice into segments to serve.

> **Frittata options**
> Try any of these combinations – or make up your own!
>
> Smoked salmon, feta and fresh dill
> Bacon and cheddar
> Red pepper, feta and olive
> Chorizo and potato
> Pea and mint
> Ham, leek and courgette
> Bacon, spinach and tomato
> Roast peppers

Serves
6

SWEET POTATO PARMAGIANA

Parmigiana can be found all over Italy, and most regions lay claim to it. There are a number of variations, but aubergine is almost always the core component. I've played around with using a few different ingredients and found thin slices of sweet potato work beautifully in place of the aubergine. Actually, I prefer it to the traditional aubergine version. Some cook this as one big dish, like a lasagne, while others cook smaller individual portions – both work well.

Ingredients

4 large sweet potatoes, peeled
Fresh basil leaves
500ml simple pomodoro sauce (see page 50) or passata
2–3 mozzarella balls
Parmesan cheese, grated
Freshly ground black pepper

Method

ROASTING – 160-200°C

Slice the sweet potatoes so that they are 5mm thick (a mandolin makes light work of this). Build up towers (aim for three or four layers of each ingredient per tower) in a baking dish with layers in the following order:

Sweet potato layer
Basil leaf
1 tbsp pomodoro sauce
Thin slice of mozzarella

Sprinkle each tower with a very generous topping of Parmesan and a grinding of black pepper. Bake for 15–20 minutes in a medium oven until the tops are browned.

You can serve this hot straight from the oven or allow it to cool and serve chilled from the fridge on a hot day.

For the traditional aubergine version:

Slice 3–4 aubergines to about 1.5cm thick rounds, discarding the ends.

Drizzle with olive oil, salt and black pepper, then slide into a hot oven for a few minutes. Don't overcook, as charred or burnt aubergine is unpleasant. As an alternative to grilling them, dust each slice in seasoned flour, dip in beaten egg and fry gently on each side.

Allow to cool on paper towels before assembling the towers, as above.

Serves
4

TACOS DE CARNITAS

This is a flavour-packed dish of slow-braised Mexican pork shoulder, marinated for 24 hours prior to cooking. It's a great one to feed a crowd as everything can be prepped in advance, meaning all you need to do is assemble the tacos on the day. Don't feel tied to just tacos – this meat is great in burritos, stews and even for topping pizzas.

Ingredients

1kg pork shoulder, cut into
  5cm pieces
4 garlic cloves, crushed
1 bay leaf
250ml freshly squeezed
  lime juice
1½ tsp Maldon sea salt
2 oranges, sliced
200ml olive oil
200g lard
1 bottle (375ml) of Mexican
  lager
1 can condensed milk
16 x 12cm corn tortillas
1 small white onion, diced
Handful of fresh coriander,
  chopped
2 limes, cut into 8 wedges,
  to serve

Method

 LOW AND SLOW – 120–160°C

First, marinate the pork by putting it into a large zip-lock bag with the garlic, bay leaf, 75ml of the lime juice, salt and orange slices. Expel all the air and zip the bag shut. Give the pork a good massage, then refrigerate for 24 hours.

Add the oil, lard, beer, condensed milk and the remaining lime juice to a large Dutch oven-style pot (or similar) and bring up to the boil.

Gently lower in the pork (after discarding its juices), cover with the lid and place near the opening of the oven for 2.5–3 hours to very gently simmer.

Once the pork is lovely and fall-apart-tender, shred it using two forks and return it to the cooking liquid.

You are now ready to assemble the tacos. Heat the tortillas for a few seconds directly on the oven floor. Put 1½ tablespoons of shredded pork in the middle, top with salsa verde or pico de gallo (see page 112), a sprinkle of onion and a pinch of coriander. Serve with lime wedges on the side.

Serves
4

CHICKEN TACOS WITH PICO DE GALLO

Ingredients

12 boneless, skinless
   chicken thighs
Taco seasoning (see below)
Olive oil, for greasing
18 (12cm) corn tortillas
Fresh coriander, chopped
2 limes, cut into 8 wedges,
   to serve

FOR THE PICO DE GALLO

1 small white onion,
   chopped
Handful of fresh coriander
   leaves, chopped
1 green serrano or jalapeño
   chilli, finely minced
Juice of 1 lime
4 ripe tomatoes, diced
Pinch of Maldon sea salt

Method

SIZZLING HOT – 220-300°C

Heat a skillet in the oven. Dust the chicken thighs with the taco seasoning. Wipe the base of the pan with a little oil on kitchen paper, then add the chicken thighs.

Cook hot and fast for about 20 minutes, turning regularly until the outside begins to char and the internal temperature of the meat reaches 75°C. Chop the chicken into small pieces.

Mix all the pico de gallo ingredients together in a separate bowl.

Heat the tortillas for a few seconds directly on the oven floor, wrap in foil, then a tea towel until ready to serve.

To dish up, fill each tortilla with 1–2 tablespoons of the chicken and about 1 tablespoon of pico de gallo. Garnish with a sprinkling of fresh coriander and serve with a lime wedge.

Taco seasoning

6 tsp cumin
4 tsp sea salt, preferably Maldon
4 tsp chipotle chilli powder
2 tsp smoked paprika
1 tsp coarsely ground black pepper
½ tsp garlic powder
½ tsp oregano
½ tsp cocoa powder
Mix all the ingredients together in a bowl.

Transfer the rub to an airtight container – it will keep for up to 1 month.

Serves
6

CHICKEN ENCHILADAS

A really simple, tasty dish that makes the most of leftover chicken.

Ingredients

4 corn tortillas

500g grated Cheddar
   cheese

About 500g leftover
   chicken, shredded

Taco seasoning (see
   page 112)

FOR THE MOLE SAUCE

½ onion, finely chopped

2 cloves of garlic

2 tbsp taco seasoning (see
   page 112)

2 tbsp cocoa powder

500ml passata

250ml chicken stock

Chipotle or ancho chilli to
   pump up the heat and add
   more smokiness if you like

TO SERVE

Soured cream

Fresh coriander, chopped

Method

ROASTING – 160-200°C

Start by making the mole sauce. Gently sauté the onion and garlic, then add the remaining ingredients. Stir well to combine, then simmer for about 20 minutes. Use a stick blender to blitz to a smooth sauce.

Wrap the tortillas in a foil pouch and slide them into the oven for 10 minutes to heat up. Remove from the oven, but keep in the foil pouch and wrap in a tea towel to keep warm until you are ready to eat.

In a large bowl, combine half the cheese, all the chicken and about 200ml of the mole sauce.

Mentally divide the mixture into eight portions (I mark it out with the blunt end of a knife).

Taking one tortilla at a time, spoon a 2.5cm strip of the mixture down the centre and roll into a fat cigar shape. Carefully place into a dish, join-side down. Repeat with the remaining tortillas until all the mixture has been used up.

Top the dish of enchiladas with more sauce, about 1 tablespoon per tortilla, before sprinkling over the rest of the grated cheese.

Slide the dish into the oven and bake for 25 minutes until the cheese is golden brown and the tops of the tortillas have crisped up.

Serve with soured cream and a sprinkling of freshly chopped coriander.

Serves
4

OLD SPOT CHOPS

Wood-fired pork chops are pretty much my favourite thing to eat. The caramelisation of the surface and the way the skin and fat turn to crackling is stupendous. I like to use meat from a Gloucestershire Old Spot pig, but any good locally reared chop will taste great.

Ingredients

Two thick-cut Gloucester
Old Spot T-bone pork chops
  (about 3cm thick)
Olive oil
Meat rub (see page 123)
Large knob of butter
Splash of white wine

Method

SIZZLING HOT - 220-300°C

Rub the chops lightly with enough oil to coat them. Dust generously with the rub and refrigerate for 1 hour.

Heat a skillet in the oven, then gently lay down the chops. Cook for 6–7 minutes in total, flipping the chops every 1–2 minutes until both sides are caramelised and golden brown.

When the chops have reached 65°C, add the butter. Swirl it around until it has melted, then deglaze the pan with the wine.

Spoon the winey/buttery sauce all over the chops. Place the chops on a warm serving tray, loosely tent with foil and leave to rest for 10 minutes before serving.

Serves
2

ROAST HAM

Why do we only seem to buy a whole ham at Christmas time? It's a delight to open the fridge and see a ham in there, winking at you and inviting you to hack off a chunk or two. Wood ovens are perfect for slow roasting a ham. Aim to keep the temperature around 100°C and add smoking wood chunks as you go to give a wonderful, deep layer of smoke.

Ingredients

3–4kg raw pork joint,
  preferably leg

FOR THE BRINE
250g Maldon sea salt
250g soft brown sugar
12 whole black peppercorns
12 whole coriander seeds
1 bunch of fresh thyme
2 cloves
2 wide strips of lemon zest
2 bay leaves

FOR THE GLAZE
2tbsp Dijon mustard
2tbsp runny honey
  juice of ½ an orange
15 cloves

Method

ROASTING - 160–200°C

Heat 6 litres of water in a large saucepan and stir in the salt and sugar until dissolved. Remove from heat, add the remaining ingredients and leave to cool.

Add the pork to the pan, ensuring it is submerged, and refrigerate for 48 hours.

Remove the pork from the brine and refrigerate, uncovered, overnight.

Place the ham in a large roasting dish and slide into the oven for 4–5 hours. Careful temperature control is required here, adding just a small piece of wood at a time.

Thirty minutes before the end of cooking, slide the ham out of the oven and carefully remove the skin; it should come away pretty easily with the help of a sharp knife. Discard the skin.

Mark the remaining fat on the ham with a nice criss-cross pattern, and stud a clove into each cross section.

Mix the honey, mustard and orange juice together in a bowl and brush over the meat.

Cook for a further 30 minutes, glazing another 3–4 times until the internal temperature of the meat reaches 80°C.

Note If you purchase a 'ham' or 'gammon' then this joint has already been cured and so you should skip the brining process or the meat will end up too salty to eat.

Serves
LOADS

SKILLET-ROASTED CHICKEN

Ingredients

1 small whole free-range chicken

Maldon sea salt and freshly ground black pepper

2 tbsp olive oil

500ml chicken stock

1 tsp Dijon mustard

6–8 garlic confit cloves (see page 51)

Small handful of finely chopped flat-leaf parsley

Method

ROASTING – 160-200°C

Spatchcock the chicken as described on page 123.

Now remove the wingtips and cut right down to the breastbone so that the chicken is completely split in half. Season both sides liberally with salt and black pepper.

Heat two skillets in the oven, then add the oil. When the oil is smoking, lay the chicken skin-side down and press down so as much skin as possible makes contact with the pan.

After 8–10 minutes, once the skin has browned, flip the chicken over and slide back into the oven. Roast for a further 25 minutes until cooked through (the internal temperature of the meat should reach 70°C).

When the chicken is cooked, remove it from the skillet and set aside to rest.

In the meantime, transfer all the juice from that skillet to the other and add half the stock. Slide back into the oven to simmer and reduce down for 5 minutes. Add the mustard and parsley, then whisk to combine. Add the garlic confit cloves.

Serve each person a chicken half, drizzled with the chicken juices.

Garnish with a sprinkling of parsley.

Serves
2

SIRLOIN ROAST

I've suggested sirloin here, but this works equally well for most decent cuts of beef. Rib, top rump and fillet all make for succulent, tasty roasts. My principle on meat is always to buy a smaller (and usually more expensive) piece of better-quality meat. Always buy beef from a source that you trust: a local butcher, farmers' market or online. The more they can tell you about the meat, the better. Look for a decent layer of fat and good marbling through the meat. Both will slowly melt away and give flavour and moisture to the beef as it cooks.

Ingredients

2 onions, roughly chopped

2 carrots, roughly chopped

4 potatoes, roughly chopped

2 celery sticks, roughly chopped

1kg joint of beef (allow 200g uncooked weight per person)

Maldon sea salt and freshly ground black pepper

Method

ROASTING – 160-200°C

Put all the vegetables into a large roasting dish.

Season the meat generously all over and lay it on top of the vegetables.

Roast in the oven, turning regularly until cooked to your liking (see the meat chart on page 13). Remove from the oven and leave to rest for 15 minutes, loosely tenting the dish with foil.

(Remember, the temperature of the beef will continue to rise by another 3–4 degrees once removed from the oven.)

Serves
5

TOASTIES

Ahh, the humble toastie. Just phenomenal when done well. There are as many options here as there are for pizza, but the cooking method remains the same throughout.

Ingredients

2 slices of sourdough bread

25g butter

1 tbsp yellow Ball Park or Dijon mustard

2 slices of ham

Mix of grated Cheddar, sliced Provolone and mozzarella cheeses

Method

SIZZLING HOT - 220-300°C

Heat a frying pan in the oven.

Butter one side of each slice of bread. Place one slice, butter-side down, onto a piece of baking parchment. Spread the unbuttered side with the mustard. Lay on the ham and cheese. Top with the remaining slice of bread, butter-side up.

Put the sandwich into the skillet, then slide into the oven and cook for 5–8 minutes until golden and crispy on both sides. (You shouldn't need to flip the sandwich over as the heat bouncing from the roof of the oven will act like a grill, meaning both sides cook at once.)

Toastie options
Try any of these combinations – or make up your own!

Bacon, egg and maple syrup
Gouda and roasted red peppers
Turkey, cranberry and stuffing
Gruyère, ham and pineapple
'Nduja and mozzarella
Ham hock and Cheddar
Mortadella and mascarpone

Serves
1

WOOD-FIRED MEAT RAGU

Ingredients

1 large onion, finely diced

1 medium carrot, finely
   diced

1 celery stick, finely diced

6 garlic cloves, minced

500g beef mince (10% fat)

500g pork mince

1 bottle (75cl) red wine

2 tbsp tomato purée

1 litre passata or chopped
   tomatoes

1 litre water or beef stock

Handful of finely chopped
   fresh sage or 2 tbsp dried
   sage

Maldon sea salt and freshly
   ground black pepper

Method

LOW AND SLOW - 120–160°C

In a large pot, sauté the onion, carrot, celery and garlic until soft.

Add the meat, season well and cook through until it is browned all over and starts to stick to the bottom of the pan when stirred.

Pour in the wine and return to the oven for 45 minutes–1 hour until it has all evaporated.

Add the tomato purée and stir well. Add the remaining ingredients, stir to combine and cook in a low oven for a minimum of 3 hours, and anything up to 6 hours.

Serves
8

ROAST CHICKEN

There's no escaping the fact that many wood-fired ovens, more often the modest-sized, garden-friendly models, have small openings that are usually designed to accommodate pizza. This restricts the dishes you can cook and larger meats, such as chicken, can be a problem.

A great way around this is to spatchcock (or butterfly) the chicken. This is done by removing the backbone and then unfolding, flattening the bird out. Not only does this allow you to cook the full roast in a smaller wood oven, but it's actually a terrific way to cook the bird as it's the same thickness throughout, meaning it cooks uniformly and remains super-moist and tender.

My best ever go-to roast chicken recipe is one from Simon Hopkinson that relies on covering the whole bird in butter and stuffing herbs inside. I've rarely cooked a Sunday roast any other way since then and I've incorporated that technique here because it adds so much flavour and succulence.

Ingredients

1 large, free-range chicken
125g butter
Meat rub (see page 131)
Juice of 1 lemon
A few sprigs of thyme and tarragon tied together into a bouquet garni with a few bay leaves

Method

ROASTING – 160–200°C

First of all, spatchcock the chicken (see box below).

Cover the skin side with the butter, season generously with meat rub, then squeeze over the lemon juice.

Heat a flat-bottomed dish in the oven and add the herb bundle. Lay the chicken, bone-side down, on top of the herbs and slide into the oven. Cook for about 25 minutes, then carefully flip the bird over and return to the oven.

Twenty minutes later, flip the bird again and return to the oven for a further 15 minutes until cooked through.

Remove the bird from the oven, pour over the juices and allow to rest for 15 minutes before serving.

> **Top tip** To spatchcock a chicken, put it breast-side down with its legs towards you. Using poultry shears or a sharp knife, carefully cut down either side of the backbone to remove it. Open the chicken out like a butterfly and turn it over. With the heel of your palm, flatten the breastbone so that the chicken is roughly the same thickness all over.

Serves 4

SPAGHETTI WITH OVEN-ROASTED TOMATOES

Ingredients

2 tbsp olive oil

8 garlic cloves, unpeeled

2kg fresh, ripe cherry
  tomatoes, halved

3–4 sprigs of fresh thyme

2 bay leaves

1 tbsp chilli flakes (optional)

1kg dried spaghetti

Handful of fresh basil leaves

Maldon sea salt and freshly
  ground black pepper

Freshly grated Parmesan
  cheese, to serve

Method

SIZZLING HOT - 220-300°C

Heat a dish in the oven. Add the oil, then the garlic and return to the oven for 5 minutes.

Add the tomatoes, thyme, bay leaves and chilli flakes (if you are using them) to the dish, season well with salt and pepper and return to the oven for 25–30 minutes. Remove from the oven and allow to cool.

Meanwhile, cook the spaghetti as per the pack instructions.

Discard the garlic cloves, thyme and bay leaves. Mix in half the basil. At this point, you can blend to a smooth sauce or keep it chunky and rustic – it's all down to personal preference!

Drain the spaghetti, transfer to a serving bowl and stir in the tomatoes. Sprinkle over the remaining basil leaves and serve with Parmesan.

Serves
6

SIMPLE PORCHETTA

A proper porchetta is something to behold. It's a whole pork belly, seasoned and rubbed with all kinds of wonderful aromatics and then wrapped round an entire pork loin. The whole thing weighs as much as a small child. Traditionally, this classic Italian roast would have been cooked in the huge, communal village wood oven for several hours and be the centrepiece for families and friends to gather and feast together. Just heaven. As wondrous as it is, you need a massive oven and about 25 people to even attempt a whole porchetta. This recipe takes much of what I love about porchetta, but turns it into a manageable Sunday roast!

Ingredients

1 skin-on pork loin, weighing about 3kg (or use half if fewer people)

50g Maldon sea salt and 2 tsp fine sea salt

2 tsp freshly ground black pepper

2 tbsp fennel seeds

50g fresh fennel tops, finely chopped

2 tbsp fresh rosemary, finely chopped

2 tbsp fresh thyme, finely chopped

2 tbsp fresh sage, finely chopped

6 garlic cloves, minced

Zest of 1 orange

Zest of 1 lemon

Method

ROASTING - 160-200°C

Using a sharp knife, carefully remove the skin from the pork loin and set aside. Butterfly the meat out. It's easy to do, but Google this first if you have never seen it done.

Lay the butterflied loin out flat in front of you. Mix the rest of the ingredients, except the fine salt, together in a bowl, then rub the herby spice mix all over.

Roll the meat up tightly into a large Swiss roll. Lay the roll on top of the reserved skin and wrap the skin around it, covering as much of the loin as you can.

Tie every 4cm with butcher's string or catering elastic bands. Rub the outside of the skin with the fine salt to help create the crackling.

Roast in a medium oven for about 1 hour until the internal temperature of the meat hits 65°C.

Serves
10

HALF A LAMB

I first cooked this recipe in Puglia many years ago in a huge outdoor wood-fired oven for about a dozen people. The Pugliese are not huge lovers of lamb though. Walk into any local village *macelleria* (butcher's) and the counter will be well stocked with beef, pork, poultry and horse. They'll have lamb, but for some reason it's one of those things you have to ask for with a nod and a wink and then wait while they disappear into a back room. In my dodgy Italian, I asked for the butcher to cut it into pieces for me. What I hoped for would be a leg, a shoulder and the rack of ribs. He misunderstood and cartoon-style chopped the whole thing into fist-size pieces with a massive knife. As it turned out, this worked really well, allowing lots of surface area to char and caramelise as the lamb cooked.

This is rustic, delicious and a great dish for a large group. It's communal cooking and dining at its best, with everyone chopping and prepping the food together, watching it cook and then sitting down to enjoy the fruits of their labour with a few glasses of the local vino.

Ingredients   ## *Method*   ROASTING – 160–200°C

½ lamb, chopped into
  fist-size pieces
12 garlic cloves, left whole
  and unpeeled
Fresh oregano
Fresh rosemary
½ bottle white wine
350ml water
Maldon sea salt and freshly
  ground black pepper

Add all the ingredients to a large roasting tray. Season well and slide into a low–medium oven. Roast for 1.5–2 hours until the liquid has reduced by half and the lamb is cooked through.

Serve with dauphinoise potatoes (see page 156), roast roots (see page 160), or any roasted vegetables.

Serves
8–10

HASSELBACK CHICKEN

Here's a recipe that is much easier to prepare than regular stuffed chicken breasts.

It cooks quickly, looks great and imparts loads of flavour to the chicken too. My kids love it!

Ingredients

2 handfuls of spinach leaves

150g ricotta cheese

Maldon sea salt and freshly
  ground black pepper

2 large free-range chicken
  breasts

50g Parmesan cheese

50g breadcrumbs

A handful of fresh basil,
  finely chopped

Method

ROASTING – 160-200°C

Wilt the spinach in a dish, chop finely and mix in the ricotta and chopped basil with a pinch of salt and black pepper.

Cut vertical slits into the chicken breasts, about 1cm apart and three-quarters of the way through the chicken. Don't cut all the way through!

Smear the spinach and ricotta mixture into the slits. Sprinkle the top with the Parmesan and breadcrumbs.

Slide the dish into the oven and bake for 20–25 minutes, until the cheese has melted, the breadcrumbs are golden and the chicken juices run clear.

Try a few variations on this dish and stuff the chicken with:

Mozzarella cheese and sundried tomatoes
Kale and goat's cheese
Boursin garlic & herbs
Chorizo and Cheddar cheese
Roasted red pepper (from a jar) and ricotta

Serves
2

ROAST RACK OF PORK

A tasty way to cook vegetables is underneath a roasting joint of meat. All the lovely fat and juices drop down and baste the vegetables, imparting a wonderful flavour. There are a couple of ways I like to do the pork. One is to cook all the accompanying vegetables underneath in a one-dish-does-all kind of way; the other is to throw in a load of Bramley apples and make a delicious apple sauce that incorporates all the meat juices. The Maldon sea salt on the skin will give a lovely crisp crackling. If you fear for your teeth and have no interest in that, then you can skip that step. Having said that, wood-fired pork crackling is nothing short of food of the gods and is well worth losing a tooth or two over.

Ingredients

2–3 tbsp fine salt
1½kg pork loin rack

FOR THE VEGETABLES
2–3 carrots, peeled and
   chopped into chunks
1 onion, cut into 8 segments
250g new or Charlotte
   potatoes, peeled and
   halved
3 celery sticks, trimmed and
   cut into chunks
Or . . .
1kg Bramley apples, peeled,
   cored and quartered
25g caster sugar
50g butter

Method

ROASTING – 160–200°C

Sprinkle the salt onto a chopping board, score the pork skin and roll onto the salt, pressing down well.

Place either the vegetables or the apples in a roasting dish. Place the pork on a rack in the dish and slide into the oven for about 1 hour until the internal temperature of the meat hits 65°C.

Remove the pork and leave to stand for 10 minutes before carving, while you dish up the vegetables or smash up the apples to make apple sauce.

Apple sauce

225g cooking apples, peeled, cored and chopped
Zest and juice of ½ lemon
2 tbsp water
15g butter
1 tsp caster sugar

Put the apples in a saucepan with the lemon juice and zest, and water.

Cover and cook over a low heat until they are soft and mushy.

Take off the heat and beat in the butter and the sugar. Cool.

Serves
4

BRAISED BEEF RIBS

Delicious, melt-in-the-mouth beef ribs with a wonderful wood-smoke flavour. The cook time for the ribs can vary hugely, so base it on the internal temperature of the meat rather than the number of hours it has been cooking.

Ingredients

About 2 racks of beef short ribs
Maldon sea salt and freshly ground black pepper
250ml beef stock

Method

 LOW AND SLOW - 120–160°C

Remove the tough membrane from the bone side of the ribs and trim off any excess fat or scraggy bits of meat.

Season generously with salt and black pepper, then place in a roasting dish, bone-side down. Add half the stock and slide into the oven.

After 2–3 hours, remove from the oven, pour in the remaining stock and tent loosely with foil. Return to the oven for a further 2 hours. Remove the foil and return to the oven for another hour or so until cooked through.

Meat/Beef rub

6 tbsp sea salt, preferably Maldon
6 tsp coarsely ground black pepper
3 tsp garlic powder
3 tsp celery salt
1½ tsp oregano

Mix all the ingredients together in a bowl.

Transfer the rub to an airtight container – it will keep for up to 1 month.

Serves
4

ROLLED BUTTERFLIED LEG OF LAMB

Leg of lamb is such a versatile joint to cook. It's happy being roasted hot and fast, giving a lovely bark on the outside and juicy, pink meat in the middle. It's also very happy being slow-cooked for hours until the meat falls from the bone and shreds with nothing more than the back of a spoon.

It's a robust-tasting meat and can stand up to some pretty powerful accompanying flavours. This recipe calls for the joint to be butterflied, which is easy enough to do yourself, but any good butcher will happily do for you. You want the meat to open up like a book, with the bones removed, into a single 'sheet' 2.5–4cm thick.

Next, get creative! The options are endless here, and once you have mastered the technique, just go for it. The idea is to spread the inside (non-skin side) of the meat with whatever you fancy – dry rubs and pastes work best. Then the lamb is rolled up like a big Swiss roll and tied up with butcher's string.

Ingredients

1 whole leg of lamb,
  butterflied and bones
  removed
1 onion, roughly chopped
2 sticks celery, roughly
  chopped
2 carrots, roughly chopped

FOR THE PASTE
5 anchovies
2 tbsp capers, drained
2 tbsp Dijon mustard
50ml olive oil
Maldon sea salt and freshly
  ground black pepper
3 sprigs of fresh rosemary
4 garlic cloves, crushed
Juice of 1 lemon

Method

ROASTING – 160-200°C

Add all the paste ingredients to a food blender and blitz into a paste, adding a little more oil if it looks too thick.

Smear the paste liberally all over the non-skin side of the butterflied leg of lamb. Roll it up like a Swiss roll and tie every 4cm with butcher's string or heatproof elastic ties.

Add the chopped veg to a roasting dish then lay the lamb on top and slide into a medium oven. Roast for about 1.5 hours until the internal temperature of the meat hits 65°C.

Other stuffing combinations

Try stuffing with the tandoori paste mix (page 134), or go Italian with the porchetta stuffing mix (page 126).

Serves
6-8

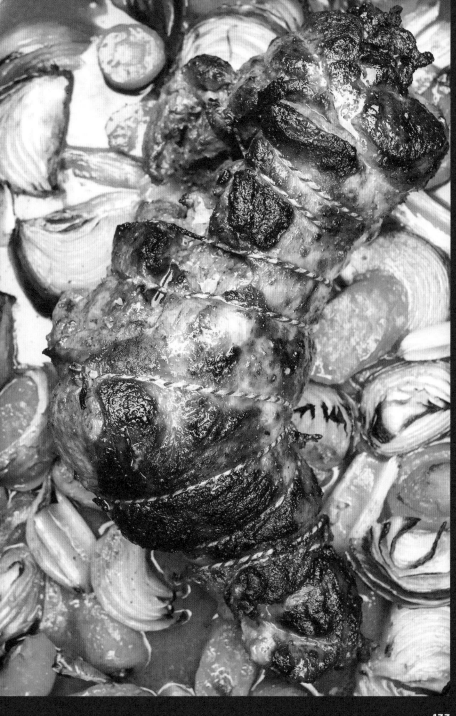

TANDOORI ROASTED CHICKEN

If your wood oven entrance doesn't allow the bird to be cooked whole, you can either spatchcock it flat (page 123) or joint into a number of smaller pieces.

Ingredients

1 large organic or free-range chicken

3 tsp tandoori masala

1 tsp coriander powder

3 tsp Kashmir chilli powder

1 tsp smoked paprika

1 tsp sea salt

2 tsp grated garlic

2 tsp grated ginger

Juice of 1 lime

3 tsp olive oil

Method

ROASTING - 160-200°C

In a bowl, mix all the spices with the garlic, ginger, lime juice and oil into a paste and rub on the inside and outside of the chicken. Leave to marinate for 1 hour.

Set your oven running at a good roasting heat and then line a roasting tin with baking parchment. Place the marinated chicken in the tin, cover loosely with foil and slide into a medium oven. Roast for 1.5 hours.

When cooked, fire up the oven to sizzling and slide the chicken back in to cook each side for 5–6 minutes until the skin is crisp.

Serves
6

JERK PORK TENDERLOINS

Ingredients

3 pork tenderloins

FOR THE JERK PASTE

Juice of 2 limes

1 tsp salt

1 scotch bonnet, finely
minced

1 tsp ground allspice

1 tsp brown sugar

1 tsp ground nutmeg

1 tsp freshly ground black
pepper

1cm piece fresh ginger,
peeled and grated

½ tsp ground cinnamon

1 garlic clove, minced

Leaves from 2–3 sprigs of
thyme

Olive oil, for greasing

Method

ROASTING - 160-200°C

Put all the jerk paste ingredients in a food blender and blitz until smooth.

Tidy up the pork tenderloins and carefully trim off any silverskin membranes.

Put the tenderloins in a zip-lock bag along with the jerk paste and massage together well. Refrigerate for 5–6 hours, removing from the fridge about 30 minutes before you start cooking.

Heat a skillet in the oven. Wipe the base with a little oil on kitchen paper, then add the pork tenderloins.

Slide into the oven and roast until golden brown and the internal temperature of the meat hits 65°C. Loosely tent the pan with foil and leave to rest for 5–10 minutes before slicing.

Serves
4-6

STEWS & ONE-POTS

CHILLI

Ideally, add a fist-sized hunk of smoking wood to the embers every 45 minutes or so to give the chilli a deep, heady, smoky aroma.

Ingredients

50g butter

1 large onion, diced

50g chilli dry mix
  (see below)

500ml chicken or beef stock

400g can chopped
  tomatoes

1 tbsp tomato purée

4 tbsp treacle

500g leftover cooked beef,
  diced to 1cm cubes, or
  750g stewing steak, or
  750g beef mince

400g can kidney beans,
  drained and rinsed

Method

LOW AND SLOW - 120–160°C

Melt the butter in a large pot, then sauté the onion until soft. Add the remaining ingredients to the pot and bring to a simmer.

Cook slowly for 2–3 hours, ideally adding a hunk of smoking wood about every 30 minutes.

To make this dish vegetarian, use 750g of chopped butternut squash instead of the meat, and vegetable stock, and cook for 30 minutes.

Chilli dry mix

2 tbsp cumin
2 tbsp diced/shredded chipotle
1 tbsp chilli flakes
1 tbsp cocoa
½ tbsp brown sugar
½ tbsp smoked salt
½ tbsp coriander
½ tbsp oregano
¼ tbsp paprika
¼ tbsp smoked paprika
¼ tbsp black pepper
1 tsp cinnamon

Mix all the ingredients together in a bowl.

Transfer the rub to an airtight container – it will keep for up to 1 month.

Serves
4-6

BEEF BARBACOA

To prepare traditional Mexican or Caribbean barbacoa you'd be expected to dig a large pit in the ground, light a massive fire in it and when the flames have died down to embers, you'd chuck in a whole sheep or goat, cover it in leaves and slow cook it for several hours. Sounds like a fun weekend to me, but I'm not sure my wife would be too happy about the massive pit in the garden. Much easier is to use our lovely wood oven to recreate the end result. We're braising the meat in a tasty, punchy Mexican broth to add to the wood smoke flavour.

Ingredients

2 tbsp beef dripping

6 medium garlic cloves, crushed

1 small onion, finely sliced

1 tbsp ancho chilli powder

4 chipotle chillies packed in adobo, roughly chopped, with 2 tbsp adobo sauce, or 4 tbsp chipotle paste

2 tsp ground cumin

½ tsp ground cloves

2 bay leaves

2 tsp dried oregano

2–2½kg beef brisket, chuck or boneless short rib, kept whole

500ml beef stock

Maldon sea salt and freshly ground black pepper

Method

LOW AND SLOW - 120–160°C

Add the beef dripping, garlic and onion to a large Dutch oven-style pot (or similar) and cook until softened.

Add the ancho chilli powder, chipotle chillies, cumin, cloves, bay leaves and oregano to the pot and cook for 1–2 minutes until the flavours are released.

Stir in the beef, then add the stock and season with salt and black pepper. Bring to the boil, then cover with a lid and cook gently for about 4 hours until the beef is very tender and pulls apart easily.

Remove the beef from the pot and reduce any remaining juices for 5 minutes. Shred the meat and mix back in with the cooking juices.

Serve with warm corn tortillas and a selection of your favourite condiments.

To serve
Warm corn tortillas
Onions
Coriander
Salsa
Limes

CHICKEN PIECES IN WINE & THYME

I'm a big fan of buying a whole chicken and chopping it into pieces at home. It's much more economical than buying it already jointed, and everyone gets to choose the cut of the bird they prefer. By all means substitute with 8–10 chicken thighs if you prefer.

Ingredients

1 whole chicken

Maldon sea salt and freshly ground black pepper

Plain flour, for dusting

2 tbsp beef dripping or olive oil

1 onion, chopped

2 celery sticks, sliced

1 fennel bulb, thinly sliced

3–4 sprigs of fresh thyme

200ml white wine

250ml good-quality chicken stock

Method

ROASTING – 160-200°C

Heat a dish in the oven. Joint the chicken into eight bone-in pieces (Google this: there are tons of great videos online). Season the pieces with salt and black pepper, then dust with flour.

Add the beef dripping or olive oil to the dish and place the chicken pieces skin-side down. Slide back into the oven and sear for about 5 minutes, then turn the chicken pieces over to sear the other side.

Remove the chicken pieces from the dish and set aside.

Add the vegetables and thyme to the dish and cook to soften. Return the chicken pieces to the dish, skin-side up, and pour over the wine. Slide back into the oven for a few minutes.

When the wine has almost cooked out, add the stock so that the chicken pieces are half submerged, but don't cover the skin. Slide back into the oven and cook for a further 25–30 minutes until the chicken is cooked through and the sauce has reduced by about half.

Serve straight from the dish, giving each person a piece of chicken, an assortment of vegetables and plenty of the delicious juice. Great with a big pile of mashed potatoes.

> **Top tip** To turn this recipe into a classic chicken chasseur, swap out the celery and fennel and instead cook down a couple of cloves of garlic and 300g button mushrooms with the onion. Stir in 1 tablespoon of tomato purée with the vegetables, too, and add about 200g of canned chopped tomatoes with the stock. Garnish with finely chopped flat-leaf parsley.

Serves 4

CASSOULET WITH DUCK LEGS

This is a dish that I've always loved and is made better in every way by being cooked in a wood oven. That extra layer of smokiness really works with the smoky pancetta. You want the duck legs to be fall-off-the-bone by the time this dish is ready to be served. The tender succulent meat should soak up all the lovely cassoulet juices. A mouthful of classic French heaven.

Ingredients

Method

ROASTING - 160-200°C

FOR THE CASSOULET
2 tbsp olive oil or goose fat
300g pancetta or
  thick-cut smoked streaky
  bacon, chopped into small
  lardons
1 small onion, roughly diced
1 large carrot, roughly diced
1 celery stick, sliced
6 garlic cloves, peeled but
  left whole
300g French garlic sausage,
  cut into 1cm slices
600g dried haricot beans,
  soaked overnight, or 3 x
  400g cans haricot beans,
  drained and rinsed
2 bay leaves
3 sprigs of fresh thyme
Finely chopped parsley, to
  garnish

FOR THE CONFIT DUCK
LEGS
6 duck leg and thigh joints
Maldon sea salt and freshly
  ground black pepper
About 500g goose or duck
  fat

Start by making the confit duck legs. Season the duck liberally with salt and black pepper and refrigerate overnight in an ovenproof dish. The next day, brush off the rub and wipe clean with kitchen paper.

Cover the duck with the fat and slide the dish into a low oven. Cook for about 2.5 hours until the meat falls off the bone. When cooked, store by placing in a bowl and covering with the fat.

To make the cassoulet, place the oil or goose fat in a dish, then add the lardons. Place near the opening of the oven and sauté for 5 minutes at a low heat until the fat starts to render.

Add the onion, carrot and celery to the dish along with the garlic and cook for a further 5 minutes. Add the sausage, beans, bay and thyme, and then pour in about 1 litre of hot water. Cook, uncovered, at a low heat for about 2 hours, stirring every 30 minutes. The juices should start to thicken a little.

Now remove the duck legs from the fridge and put them into a separate dish, skin-side up.

Slide into the oven for 30–40 minutes until the skin is crisp. The internal temperature should reach about 75°C.

To serve, ladle a generous helping of cassoulet into bowls, place a duck leg on top and garnish with parsley.

Serves
6

LANCASHIRE HOTPOT

I grew up on the Pennine Way in Lancashire, and the field directly in front of our house was used by the local farmer to graze sheep, as were most fields in the area. Sunday roasts were always leg of lamb with lots of rosemary and mint sauce. It was a lamb town and I loved it. One of my all-time favourite dishes was Lancashire hotpot, although we didn't call it that, just hotpot. It's a great dish to prepare in advance and just slide into the oven when your guests arrive.

Ingredients

Beef dripping or olive oil

1kg stewing lamb, cut into bite-size chunks

2 onions, chopped

1 celery stick, sliced

4 carrots, roughly chopped

2 tbsp plain flour

Salt and freshly ground black pepper

500ml lamb or beef stock

1kg potatoes, peeled and cut into 2–3mm thick slices

Pickled red cabbage, to serve

Method

LOW AND SLOW - 120–160°C

Heat a dish in a medium oven and add a good tablespoon of beef dripping. Sear the lamb in batches so as not to crowd the dish as it needs space to brown properly. Transfer the batches of lamb to a handy bowl while you sear the next lot.

Tip in the vegetables with a little more dripping and cook until softened. Sprinkle over the flour, season with salt and black pepper, and combine well.

Pour in the stock, stir in the lamb, then layer the potatoes over the top. Cover loosely with foil and slide back into the oven for about 1.5 hours until you can insert the blade of a sharp knife easily through the potato lid.

Remove the foil, brush with more dripping and return to the oven for a further 10–15 minutes until beautifully browned. Serve with pickled red cabbage.

Serves 8

BRUNSWICK STEW

One that harks back to my barbecue days, Brunswick stew is a thick vegetable stew-with shredded meat all cooked up together slowly in a large pot. I imagine it started out life as a hunter's dish, giving them a way to use up leftover game. Now though, next time you have a big cook out and have lots of leftover meat, this is the dish for you. Quick and simple to prepare, the dish tastes best using meats that have been cooked in the wood oven so they retain the lovely smoky flavours. If not, add 1 tablespoon of sweet smoked paprika to bring in the smoky note.

Ingredients

50g butter
1 large onion, diced
1 red pepper, diced
3 large potatoes, peeled and
  diced into 1cm cubes
½ tsp cayenne pepper
½ tbsp freshly ground black
  pepper
½ tbsp salt
1 tsp smoked sweet paprika
  (optional)
15ml Worcestershire sauce
5 splashes of Tabasco/hot
  sauce
2 x 400g cans chopped
  tomatoes
500ml chicken stock
500g frozen sweetcorn
500g canned cannellini
beans, drained and rinsed
1.5kg leftover chopped/
  shredded meat

Method

ROASTING - 160-200°C

Melt the butter in a large Dutch oven-style pot (or similar), then sauté the onion and red pepper.

Add the remaining ingredients, stir well and bring to a simmer.

Cook gently for about 30 minutes until the potatoes are cooked through and the liquid has thickened.

> **Top tip** By all means accumulate leftover meat over a number of weeks. Just shred or chop it up and keep adding it to a food bag in the freezer until you have enough for a big batch of stew.

Serves
6-8

RIBOLLITA

Some of my favourite ever Italian dishes transform humble ingredients and leftovers into a flavour-packed, hearty and comforting dish – peasant food to nourish and warm the cockles of your heart after a hard day on the land. Ribollita (meaning 'reboiled') is just that, incorporating store-cupboard basics and stale bread into a rich, thick soup that is a pleasure to cook and beautifully colourful. A bowlful of Tuscany.

Ingredients

Generous glug of olive oil,
plus extra to serve

1 large onion, chopped

2 carrots, diced

3 celery sticks, sliced

3 garlic cloves, crushed

150g thick-cut smoked
bacon or pancetta, diced
(optional)

500ml chicken or vegetable
stock

400g can chopped
tomatoes

400g can cannellini beans,
drained and rinsed

2 sprigs of fresh thyme

2 sprigs of fresh rosemary

Maldon sea salt and freshly
ground black pepper

300g cavolo nero leaves or
dark savoy cabbage, finely
shredded

6 slices of sourdough bread,
preferably a few days old

Handful of fresh basil,
chopped

Method

ROASTING - 160-200°C

Add the oil to a large dish, then add the onion, carrots, celery and garlic (and bacon, if using). Sauté for 5–10 minutes until softened.

Add the stock, tomatoes, beans and herbs and bring to a simmer.

Season well with salt and black pepper. Cook for about 20 minutes, then add the cavolo nero and cook for a further 15 minutes.

Lay a slice of bread in each bowl, fill with the ribollita and top with a drizzle of good-quality olive oil and a sprinkle of basil.

> **Top tip** There is no single 'right' way to make ribollita. By its very nature it is a dish that uses up whatever you have in the cupboard. The main ingredients of leftover bread, beans and a dark cabbage are usually present, but after that it's up to you. Try it with leeks, potato, chard, squash, olives, chilli, etc. Go with the flow and embrace your inner Italian donna.

Serves
6

BEEF BOURGUIGNON WITH VICHY CARROTS

Ingredients

3 tbsp beef dripping

600g shin beef, cut into
  large chunks

Plain flour, for dusting

1 bottle (75cl) red wine,
  preferably Burgundy

100g smoked streaky
  bacon, sliced, or lardons

350g shallots, peeled and
  left whole

2 garlic cloves, crushed

2 bay leaves

2 sprigs of fresh thyme

250g button mushrooms

1 tbsp tomato purée

Small handful of finely
  chopped parsley

FOR THE CARROTS

500g carrots, peeled,
  topped and tailed

50g butter

50g caster sugar

Maldon sea salt

Method

LOW AND SLOW - 120–160°C

Start with the beef. Add 2 tbsp of the beef dripping to a large dish and heat. Dust the beef chunks with flour and fry in batches until browned. Transfer the beef to a bowl and deglaze the dish with a slosh of red wine and scrape all the burnt bits off. Pour the deglaze juice into a separate bowl for use later.

Add remaining beef dripping to the dish, then add the bacon, shallots, garlic, bay leaves, thyme and mushrooms. Sauté for about 5 minutes, then stir in the tomato purée.

Add the beef back in the dish along with the reserved juices and the rest of the red wine.

Cover and cook for 2–2.5 hours. Garnish with parsley.

For the carrots, add them whole to a dish and just cover with water.

Add the butter, sugar and a pinch of salt. Cover and slide into the oven for 45 minutes–1 hour until most of the liquid has evaporated and the carrots are very tender.

Great served with a big pile of mash or layered potatoes (see page 156).

Serves
4-6

SPICY CHORIZO SOUP

A hearty winter warmer. Serve with rustic bread.

Ingredients

1 tbsp olive oil

4 celery sticks, cut into 1cm
   slices

1 large onion, finely chopped

3 garlic cloves, crushed

1 tsp oregano

1 tsp dried ancho chilli

Handful of chestnut mush
   rooms, halved

240g chorizo, chopped into
   bite-size chunks

500ml vegetable stock

800g passata

400g butter beans,
   drained and rinsed

400g borlotti beans,
   drained and rinsed

400g kidney beans,
   drained and rinsed

Small bag of baby leaf
   spinach

Crème fraîche, to serve

Method

ROASTING - 160-200°C

Add the oil to a heavy-based saucepan with the celery, onion and garlic. Sauté for about 10 minutes until nice and soft, being careful not to burn anything.

Stir in the oregano, chilli, mushrooms and chorizo and cook for a few minutes.

Add the stock, passata and all the beans. Cook at about 200°C for 20 minutes, stirring occasionally. At the very end of cooking, stir in the spinach and let it wilt.

Serve in bowls with a spoonful of crème fraîche.

Serves
6

SIDES & SHARERS

ROAST NUTS

Every pub these days has 'smoked' nuts as a bar snack, but they're generally rubbish, and are artificially smoky, even in the posh places. These are the genuine article and not much goes better with a cold beer than a bowlful of 'still-hot-from-the-wood-oven' home-smoked nuts.

Once you have the hang of it, experiment with other nut types. Almonds and cashews work very well, but are much more expensive! Also, start playing around with different seasonings, but be careful not to over-salt. Start with a small trial batch first.

Ingredients

1 egg white
500g plain, unsalted
*   blanched peanuts*
4 tbsp nut rub (see below)

Method

ROASTING - 160-200°C

Get the oven running around medium, but add in some fresh wood chunks to get some smoke going.

In a large bowl, mix the egg white into the nuts. Keep stirring until all the nuts have a glossy coating. Add the nut rub and mix well until evenly distributed.

Spread the nuts out in a single layer onto a baking tray and slide into the oven for about 10 minutes – you will need to do this in batches.

Remove the tray from the oven and mix the nuts around a bit as you'll find they have stuck together. Return to the oven for a further 5–10 minutes until golden brown all over.

Allow to cool a little, then gently break apart any clumps that have formed.

For the Nut rub

6 tbsp sea salt, preferably Maldon
1 tbsp garlic powder
1 tbsp celery salt
1½ tsp oregano
2 tbsp freshly ground black pepper

Mix all the ingredients together in a bowl.

Transfer to an airtight container where it will keep happily for up to 1 month.

Serves lots

DAUPHINOISE POTATOES

A delicious, rich, creamy and satisfying side dish.

Ingredients

500ml double cream

500ml milk

4 garlic cloves, kept whole

2 sprigs of fresh thyme

Salt and freshly ground
   black pepper

6–8 large potatoes (King
Edward or Maris Piper are
   best), peeled

Butter, for greasing

Method

ROASTING - 160-200°C

Add the cream, milk, 3 of the garlic cloves and thyme to a large saucepan and bring to a simmer. Season with a pinch of salt and black pepper.

Use a mandolin (or sharp knife) to slice the potatoes into 3–4mm discs, then add them to the hot milky mixture. Cook for a few minutes until the potatoes start to soften slightly.

Rub a 30cm dish with a garlic clove sliced in half, then with butter.

Remove the potatoes with a slotted spoon and layer them nicely in the dish. Remove the garlic cloves and thyme from the milky liquid and pour over the potatoes until they are just submerged.

Bake the dish for about 1 hour in a medium oven until the top is beautifully browned and you can easily slide a sharp knife through the potatoes.

> **Top tip** To make a slightly healthier but just as tasty version of this dish, layer the uncooked sliced potatoes straight into a dish, sprinkling some fresh thyme leaves, salt, black pepper and a drizzle of olive oil between each layer. Once the dish is full, pour in stock to around half way and drizzle the top with more olive oil. Cook as above.

Serves
6-8

ROASTED OLIVES

A quick and simple one to fling in the oven while you are cooking other things. Delicious with an ice-cold G&T.

Ingredients

Good slug of olive oil
8 garlic cloves, crushed
2 sprigs of fresh rosemary
1 dried bird's eye chilli, or
   chilli de árbol
1 bay leaf
500g mixed olives (a
   selection of colours and
   sizes looks great)
1 lemon, whole
Juice of 1 tangerine
Cracked black pepper

Method

ROASTING - 160-200°C

Heat the oil in a skillet, then add the garlic and cook for 1–2 minutes (don't let the garlic burn!).

Add the rosemary, chilli, bay leaf and olives, and move the skillet nearer the opening of the oven to a cooler spot.

Peel the lemon and add the rind to the skillet, then squeeze over the juice. Pour in the tangerine juice and season with black pepper. Roast gently for about 20 minutes, stirring regularly.

You can store the olives in an airtight container in the fridge for up to two weeks, but they are best served fresh out of the hot oven.

Serves
6-8

ROAST ROOTS

Feel free to mix this up with whatever looks good at the farmer's market. Red onions, butternut squash and beetroot all work well.

Ingredients

3 tbsp olive oil
5 medium carrots, peeled
   and cut into long slices
1 large celeriac, peeled and
   cut into chunks
5 parsnips, peeled and cut
   into long sticks
6 garlic cloves, kept whole
A few sprigs of fresh thyme
2 tbsp clear honey
2 tsp black peppercorns,
   roughly cracked
Maldon sea salt

Method

ROASTING – 160-200°C

Heat the oil in a large roasting tin, then add the roots, garlic and thyme.

Roast in the oven for about 45 minutes, giving the tin a shake every now and then.

When the roots are cooked and tender and a lovely golden colour, stir in the honey, peppercorns and a sprinkling of salt, then return to the oven for a further 5 minutes.

Serves
6-8

BABA GANOUSH

The key ingredient for baba ganoush is the mighty aubergine, originally from India, where it was grown 5000 years ago before making its way into Europe via Italy around the thirteenth century as a result of trade with the Arabs.

A heady, dense, smoky flavour makes for a wonderful baba ganoush, and blackening the vegetables in a wood oven is 100 per cent guaranteed to taste better than doing it over a gas hob. The more real-fire character you can shoehorn into the dish, the better. My brother, Bob, makes this recipe in Italy for me every summer, and I love it. It's got more going on than a regular baba ganoush, but it's worth the extra effort.

Ingredients

1 large aubergine

400g can chickpeas, drained and rinsed

2 garlic cloves, crushed

1 lemon, squeezed, plus zest

½ tsp cumin

½ tsp zaatar

½ tsp sweet smoked paprika

2 tbsp tahini

3 tbsp olive oil

Generous pinch of Maldon sea salt and freshly ground black pepper

Handful of chopped parsley and coriander

Honey, to taste (optional)

Method

SIZZLING HOT - 220-300°C

Place the aubergine in a hot oven, close to the flame so that it scorches. Keep turning it regularly until it has blackened and gone lovely and soft.

Allow to cool enough so you can handle it, then slice it open and scoop out the smoky, soft insides into a bowl. Discard the charred skin.

Smash the chickpeas with a potato masher. Mix all the remaining ingredients together (except the honey) in a large bowl with the chickpeas and aubergine flesh.

Taste for sweetness and add a little honey if needed. Drizzle a little more olive oil on top before serving.

Serves
6

KANSAS CITY BBQ BEANS

Feel free to add shredded meat from previous roasts to the pot. The more kinds you add, the richer and more complex the flavours will be.

Ingredients

A glug of beef dripping or
  olive oil
2 onions, diced
1 red pepper, diced
1 green pepper, diced
3 x 400g cans haricot
  beans, drained and rinsed
120ml your favourite
  barbecue sauce (or 90ml
  ketchup, 30ml
Worcestershire sauce, 2
  tbsp mustard powder and
100g dark brown sugar)
2 tbsp black treacle (or
  molasses if you can find it)
2 tbsp cider vinegar
½ tsp cayenne pepper
300ml dark malty beer or
  cider (not IPA)
200ml water
2 tsp barbecue seasoning
  (your own or shop bought)

Method

LOW AND SLOW - 120–160°C

Add a knob of beef dripping or glug of oil to a roasting dish and cook down the vegetables for 5 minutes until soft.

Stir in all the other ingredients.

Cook in a low oven for 2–3 hours, stirring every 30 minutes. The resulting beans should be thick and unctuous.

> **Optional** Chop 6 thick-cut bacon rashers into lardons and fry in the dish. When browned, remove from the dish and set aside. You can return the lardons to the dish when you add the beans.

Serves
4-6

ROMANESCO CHEESE

This recipe works equally well for your common or garden cauliflower. I love to use the romanesco when it is in season though – it's such a fabulous looking veg! Like some crazy infinity spiral drawn by a modern artist.

Ingredients

2 whole romanesco
  cauliflowers
40g butter
40g plain flour
500ml milk
500g strong Cheddar
  cheese, grated
Salt and white pepper

Method

ROASTING – 160-200°C

Bring a saucepan of water to the boil and add a pinch of salt.

Remove and discard the leaves from the cauliflowers and slice the whole heads in half lengthways, top to bottom through the core, so you are left with two equal halves. Add the cauliflower to the pan and simmer for 5 minutes until tender, then drain.

Butter a dish and add the cooked cauliflower, cut-side down.

Make a cheese sauce by melting the butter in a saucepan over a medium heat, then add the flour and stir well until the mixture reaches a cookie dough colour and consistency.

Add one-third of the milk and stir or whisk well until combined and lump free. Add another third of the milk and repeat. Finally, add the remaining third of the milk and keep whisking until the sauce starts to simmer.

Handful by handful, add three-quarters of the cheese and stir into the sauce until smooth then season with salt and white pepper.

Pour the sauce over the cauliflower and sprinkle the top with the remaining cheese. Bake in a medium oven for 20 minutes until the top is browned and the sauce is bubbling.

Serves
6

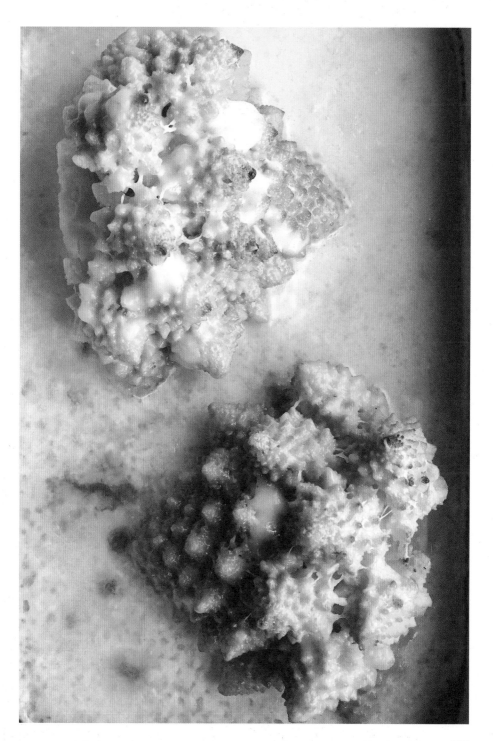

MAC 'N' CHEESE
WITH BACON DUST

Ingredients

10 rashers of good-quality
   smoked streaky bacon
1 quantity of cheese sauce
   (see page 164)
500g elbow macaroni
Splash of olive oil
Butter, for greasing
Breadcrumbs

Method

ROASTING - 160-200°C

Put the bacon on a tray and slide into the oven for about 10 minutes until cooked through and crispy.

Make a cheese sauce following the recipe on page 164.

Cook the macaroni until tender but not quite cooked through, maybe 1–2 minutes less than the packet suggests. Then drain and drizzle with oil to stop it sticking together.

Rub the inside of a 30cm dish with butter. Coarsely chop 6 slices of the bacon, then mix in with the cheese sauce and macaroni until combined. Tip into the buttered dish.

Top with breadcrumbs, then slide the dish into the oven for 30 minutes, or until the top is golden, crispy and bubbling.

Meanwhile, blitz up some very crispy bacon in a food blender (or chop very finely) and sprinkle over the top of the cooked dish before serving.

Serves
4

YORKSHIRE PUDDINGS

As a man who grew up in Lancashire, the popularity of the humble Yorkie makes me cry a little inside every time I think about it. Having said that, they accompany virtually every single roast in our house and my kids especially adore them. My father-in-law used to eat them for breakfast covered in golden syrup. Breakfast of champions if you ask me.

Everyone has their go-to recipe, but the problem is it's never 100% foolproof. My friend Martin posts photos of his attempts every Sunday, good or bad, without fail. His friends offer the dearest of praise and the harshest abuse. So don't beat yourself up; cherish the triumphs and forget the defeats. Brush yourself off and fight on another day.

Here's my 'almost' foolproof recipe.

Ingredients

300ml milk
Pinch of Maldon sea salt
3 large eggs
150g plain flour
6 tsp beef dripping

Method

ROASTING - 160-200°C

If you own a NutriBullet-style gadget, add the milk, salt and eggs, then the flour. Screw on the lid and blitz. If you don't, whisk or blend everything together to a smooth batter.

Transfer to a large jug, cover and leave the mix to chill in the fridge for at least 3 hours, or anything up to 8 hours.

With the oven running at medium, slide in a Yorkshire pudding tray, one with 12 holes, for about 15 minutes to heat up.

Remove briefly just to add ½ teaspoon of beef dripping to each hole, then slide back in until the fat is smoking hot. Pour the batter evenly into the holes and slide back into the oven.

They'll hopefully puff up into beautiful, golden, resplendent Yorkies in about 20 minutes.

Post your photos on Facebook regardless.

Makes 12

ROAST POTATOES

Everyone can cook roast potatoes. Surely one of the simplest and most widely cooked recipes in the world. But as with many things cooked in a wood oven, the real fire char and smoky hit elevate them to another level. Don't worry about a few extra-crunchy or scorched potatoes – they're the best bits!

Ingredients

2 tbsp beef dripping or goose fat

4 large Maris Piper or King Edward potatoes (based on four big roasties each)

Maldon sea salt and freshly ground black pepper

6 garlic cloves, left whole and unpeeled

2 sprigs of fresh rosemary

Method

ROASTING - 160-200°C

Put the beef dripping in a dish and slide it into a medium oven to melt and get smoking hot.

Peel and quarter the potatoes. Bring a large saucepan of water to the boil with a pinch of salt, then par-cook the spuds for about 5 minutes until they start to soften. Drain well and allow to cool slightly, letting any steam evaporate.

In a large bowl, toss together the potatoes, garlic and rosemary with another pinch of salt and a grinding or two of black pepper.

Carefully (don't let the fat splash you) tip the spuds into the dish and stir well to combine.

Slide into the oven for about 45 minutes, turning occasionally, until the outside of the potatoes is crispy and golden and the inside gives way easily when poked with a sharp knife.

Serves 4

ROASTED BEETS & FETA SALAD

Ingredients

FOR THE ROASTED BEETS
8 large fresh beetroots
(not pickled) in a variety of
colours
Splash of olive oil
1 tsp fennel seeds
1 tsp dried oregano
Maldon sea salt
Splash of cider vinegar

FOR THE SALAD
½ red onion, thinly sliced
1 whole fennel bulb, thinly
sliced
1 large orange, peeled and
cut into segments
1 block (200g) of feta
cheese, crumbled
50g toasted almonds,
chopped
50g pumpkin seeds, toasted
Fresh mint leaves, torn, to
garnish

FOR THE DRESSING
2 tsp Dijon mustard
1 tsp clear honey
2 tbsp red wine vinegar
6 tbsp olive oil

Method

ROASTING – 160–200°C

Start by making the beets. Peel the beetroots and cut them into large wedges. Put them in a bowl and toss with the oil, fennel seeds and oregano. Season with salt and the cider vinegar. Transfer to a tray and roast for 1.5 hours until tender, then allow to cool.

For the salad, arrange the onion, fennel, orange and roasted beets on a large platter. Sprinkle with the feta, almonds and pumpkin seeds.

Whisk all the dressing ingredients together in a small bowl or jar and drizzle over the salad.

Garnish with a few mint leaves.

Serves
4

ROAST FIGS WITH BACON & FETA

Ingredients

6 rashers of air-cured, thick-cut streaky bacon

12 fresh figs, halved length ways and stems removed

1 block (200g) of feta (or goat's) cheese, crumbled

Method

ROASTING – 160–200°C

Lay the bacon on a baking tray and roast until crispy, then chop it into small pieces.

Arrange the figs cut-side up on a tray.

Top each half with a little cheese and a few crumbles of bacon.

Roast until the cheese melts and the edges of the figs are golden.

BRAISED ONIONS

Ingredients

Large knob of butter
24 white pearl onions,
  peeled
200ml stock
1 sprig of fresh thyme
1 sprig of fresh rosemary
Maldon sea salt and freshly
  ground black pepper

Serves
4-6

Method

LOW AND SLOW - 120–160°C

Heat a dish in a medium oven, then add the butter. When the butter begins to froth, add the onions.

Return to the oven for about 10 minutes until the onions start to brown.

Pour in the stock, add the herbs and season with salt and black pepper. Loosely cover with foil and return to the oven for about 45 minutes.

ROAST FENNEL WITH BREADCRUMBS

Ingredients

6 fennel bulbs, stalks and
  fronds removed, quartered
  lengthways into wedges
A glug of olive oil
Fresh thyme
Maldon sea salt and freshly
  ground black pepper
500g cherry tomatoes
1 garlic clove, crushed
Handful of fresh basil,
  chopped
300g breadcrumbs
250g grated Parmesan
  cheese

Serves
6

Method

ROASTING - 160-200°C

Heat a dish in a medium oven.

In a large mixing bowl, toss the fennel wedges with the oil, along with the thyme and a generous pinch of salt and black pepper. Add to the dish and return to the oven for 10 minutes.

Turn the fennel over and cook for a further 10 minutes until softened, slightly charred and properly cooked through.

Cut the cherry tomatoes in half and sprinkle over the fennel along with the garlic and basil.

Mix the breadcrumbs with the cheese and sprinkle over the tomatoes and fennel. Return to the oven for a further 10 minutes until the top is golden brown and crispy.

ROASTED RATATOUILLE

Ingredients

2 courgettes
1 aubergine
1 green pepper
1 red pepper
1 red onion
4 garlic cloves, kept whole
2 tbsp olive oil
Splash of white wine
400g can chopped
   tomatoes, or fresh plum
   tomatoes chopped into
   chunks
250ml of stock
Fresh thyme and oregano
Maldon sea salt and freshly
   ground black pepper

Method

ROASTING – 160-200°C

Chop all the vegetables, apart from the garlic, into equal-size pieces, about 1.5cm.

Add all the vegetables and garlic to a roasting dish, drizzle over the oil and mix well. Slide into the oven for about 20 minutes until the vegetables have softened and started to char.

Add the wine and deglaze the bottom of the dish before adding the tomatoes and the stock. Stir in the herbs, season with salt and black pepper, and slide back into the oven for a further 20 minutes until the sauce has thickened up nicely.

Serves
4

ROASTED CEPS WITH THYME

Ingredients

300g fresh ceps, halved
   lengthways
2 tbsp olive oil
50g butter
2 garlic cloves, crushed
A few sprigs of fresh thyme
Juice of ½ lemon
Maldon sea salt
2 tbsp finely chopped
   parsley

Method

ROASTING - 160-200°C

Gently brush away any loose dirt from the ceps and trim off the ends of the stalks.

Heat a skillet in the oven, then add the oil. Toss the ceps around until coated and return the skillet to the oven. Cook for 10 minutes, turning every few minutes.

When the mushrooms have started to caramelise, add the butter, garlic and thyme leaves. Toss everything well and return to the oven for a further 5 minutes.

Squeeze over the lemon juice and season with salt. Finally, sprinkle over the parsley.

This is lovely served on a thick slice of toasted sourdough bread.

Also delicious as a pizza topping.

Serves
2

BOMBAY POTATOES

This recipe is far from authentic, but these Bombay potatoes are so tasty cooked in a wood oven! I mix up a big batch of the spice mix and keep it in a sealed jar as it lasts for ages.

Ingredients

Method

500g Maris Piper or
  Charlotte potatoes, peeled
  and halved
1 tsp turmeric
Splash of olive oil
2 tbsp Bombay potato spice
  mix (see below)
Small handful of chopped
  fresh coriander, to garnish

Add the potatoes and turmeric to a large saucepan and cover with water. Boil until tender, then drain. When cool enough to handle, cut into 2.5cm cubes.

In a large bowl, mix the oil, potatoes and Bombay spice mix together until the potatoes are well coated.

Heat the oil in a dish in the oven. When hot, carefully tip in the potatoes. Roast until just starting to brown and piping hot throughout.

Garnish with the coriander.

If you like, you can mix a 400g can of chickpeas, drained and rinsed, with the potatoes when they head into the oven.

Another tasty variation is to chuck in a handful of chopped spinach right at the end then allow it to wilt.

Bombay potato spice mix

2 tbsp turmeric
2 tbsp black mustard seeds
2 tbsp sesame seeds
1 tbsp garam masala
1 tbsp cumin
1 tbsp ground coriander
1 tbsp chilli flakes
1 tbsp Maldon sea salt
1 tbsp freshly ground black pepper

Mix all the ingredients together in a small bowl, then store in an airtight glass jar.

Serves
4-6

BREADS

CHAPATTIS

Here's a recipe that just could not be simpler. Absolutely perfect cooked in a raging hot wood oven and delicious, not just with Indian food, but to accompany everything! It's a go-to in our house – even brushed with butter and spread with jam for breakfast some days!

Ingredients

600g wholewheat or chapatti flour
350–400ml water
Melted butter or ghee (optional)

Method

SCREAMING HOT - 300–450°C

Add the flour to a large bowl and mix in enough water to make a lovely soft dough (or add to the bowl of a food mixer fitted with dough hook). The wetter the dough, the trickier it will be to deal with, but the softer the chapattis will be.

Knead the mixture until smooth, then cover with a tea towel and leave to stand for 30 minutes.

Tear off a piece about the size of a ping-pong ball and roll it into a ball shape. Using a rolling pin, roll the ball into a thin disc on a floured board and flip it over a couple of times during this process to make sure both sides get floured.

Slide the chapatti into a hot oven. Move it around with some long tongs until it browns, blisters and puffs up – keep your eye on it as it will cook in a matter of seconds!

Traditionally, chapattis are brushed with melted butter or ghee once cooked, but this is a matter of personal preference!

Makes 12

DOUGH BALLS

Ingredients

1 quantity of white bloomer
dough (see page 191)

Method

ROASTING – 160–200°C

Prepare the bread dough as per the instructions on page 191.

Cut the dough into 40 pieces and roll each piece between your hands into a ball.

Place the dough balls on floured baking trays and bake in batches for 8–10 minutes. You'll know they're cooked when they sound hollow when tapped on the bottom.

Use to dip in anything you like. Try the babaganoush (see page 162) or make a simple garlic butter as in the recipe on page 183.

Makes
40

GARLIC BREAD

Ingredients

1 quantity of white bloomer
dough (see page 191)

FOR THE GARLIC BUTTER

150g butter, softened
8 garlic cloves, crushed
Small handful of parsley,
finely chopped

Method

ROASTING - 160-200°C

Prepare the bread dough as per the instructions on page 191.

Form the dough into two or three long, thin baguette shapes. Once doubled in size, bake for about 20 minutes and allow to cool.

Meanwhile, make the garlic butter by mixing the butter, garlic and parsley together in a bowl.

When the baguettes are cooked, make slits all the way along each baguette at 2cm intervals, about three-quarters of the way through (don't slice all the way through!). Smear a little garlic butter into each slit, then wrap each baguette in foil and slide back into the oven for 15 minutes.

Makes
2-3 baguettes

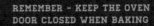

REMEMBER - KEEP THE OVEN
DOOR CLOSED WHEN BAKING

FOCACCIA

You can get all kinds of crazy with the herbs and ingredients used to flavour a focaccia. This one keeps it simple with some herbs, but try adding some wood-oven roasted onions or some garlic confit. Serve the focaccia still warm from the oven. It's wonderful to soak up the juices in big hearty stews.

Ingredients

7g sachet dried yeast

300ml warm water

75ml very good-quality olive oil

560g strong white flour, plus extra for dusting

10g salt

FOR THE TOPPING

25ml olive oil

2 tbsp mixed dried herbs (or 4 tbsp fresh rosemary and oregano)

Maldon sea salt

Method

ROASTING - 160-200°C

To make the focaccia, mix the yeast with the water and 50ml of the oil in a jug.

Add the flour and salt to a large bowl, then pour in the liquid. Mix all the ingredients together well, then tip out onto a floured surface and knead for 15 minutes. Alternatively, use a food mixer fitted with a dough hook on speed 1 for 10 minutes.

When the dough is smooth, return it to the bowl, cover with a tea towel and leave it somewhere warm for about 1 hour until it has doubled in size.

Pour the remaining 25ml of oil onto a baking tray, swirling it around so that the base is covered.

To prepare the topping, pour the oil into a small bowl along with the herbs and place at the opening of the oven to heat up (but not fry), then set aside.

Once the dough has risen, stretch it out to the shape of your baking tray, pushing the edges out. It should be about 1.5–2cm deep at this point. Cover and leave for a further hour or so until doubled in size again.

Using your fingertips, prod the dough all over, making about 30 dimples. Pour over the herby oil and sprinkle generously with salt.

Slide the tray into the oven for about 20 minutes until the top is golden brown and the bottom lifts cleanly from the tray.

Makes 1 Loaf

REMEMBER - KEEP THE OVEN DOOR CLOSED WHEN BAKING

SEED-TOPPED TEAR 'N' SHARE

Ingredients

 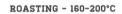

FOR THE BREAD
150ml warm full-fat milk

50ml clear honey

150ml warm water

7g sachet dried yeast

560g strong white flour

10g salt

50g soft butter

3 tbsp sunflower seeds

1 tbsp poppy seeds

2 tbsp flax seeds

FOR THE TOPPINGS
1 tbsp poppy seeds

1½ tsp sesame seeds

1 tsp fennel seeds

½ tsp Maldon sea salt

1 tsp garlic salt

1 tbsp dried oregano

2 large egg yolks, beaten

Method

Mix the milk, honey and warm water together in a jug and stir in the yeast.

Add the flour, salt and butter to the bowl of a food mixer fitted with a dough hook. Once the yeast mixture starts to foam, pour it into the flour and mix well on speed 1 for about 3 minutes.

Tip in the seeds and mix for a further 3–4 minutes until a smooth, soft dough forms.

Cover the bowl with a tea towel and leave at room temperature for 1 hour until doubled in size. Once risen, divide the dough into 16 equal pieces and shape into balls. Place the balls 1–2 cm apart in a 30cm cast-iron skillet. Cover again for about 25 minutes and allow to rise until doubled in size.

To make the topping, combine the seeds together in a small bowl with the salt, oregano and garlic salt. Brush the rolls with the beaten egg yolks and evenly sprinkle the seed mixture on top.

Slide into the oven and bake for about 25 minutes until golden brown. Let cool for 10 minutes before serving.

Makes
16 pieces

CAST-IRON POT SOURDOUGH

The best sourdough loaves are made from quite wet and sticky doughs that can be tricky to handle and move around. This method of cooking sourdough in a cast-iron pot not only helps the loaf keep its shape, but also heats it rapidly from all sides, giving a quick and impressive rise in the oven and lovely big pockets inside.

Ingredients

400g lively sourdough
   starter
650g malted bread flour,
   plus extra for dusting
475g lukewarm water
20g fine sea salt

Method

ROASTING - 160-200°C

Combine all ingredients, except the salt, in a large bowl and cover with a tea towel.

After 30 minutes, add the salt, then fold the dough once in the following way: bottom to top, left to right, top to bottom and right to left. Repeat this every 30 minutes for the next 2 hours.

Shape the dough into a ball and leave to prove in a floured banneton (or a bowl lined with a tea towel) for up to 2 hours, or until the dough doesn't fully spring back when poked (slow this down in the fridge for up to 24 hours for improved flavour).

Pop into a preheated cast-iron pot, slash with a very sharp knife, cover with a lid and bake for 30 minutes, then remove the lid and bake for a further 15 minutes.

Enjoy with loads of butter.

Recipe kindly donated by Harry Madeley (Instagram: @hmadeley).

Makes
1 loaf

**REMEMBER - KEEP THE OVEN
DOOR CLOSED WHEN BAKING**

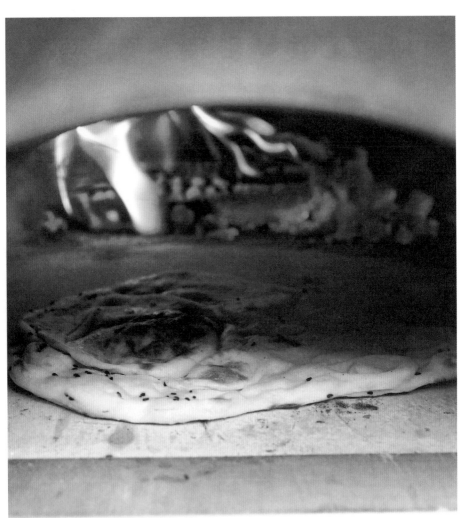

NIGELLA-SEEDS NAAN

Ingredients

100ml lukewarm water

¼ tsp dried yeast

Pinch of salt

Pinch of sugar

325g self-raising flour, plus extra for dusting

6 tsp plain yoghurt

1 tsp nigella seeds

40ml full-fat milk

4 tsp rapeseed oil

Butter, for brushing

Method

SCREAMING HOT - 300-450°C

In a bowl, mix the lukewarm water with the yeast, salt and sugar. Leave to stand for 10 minutes.

In a separate bowl, add the flour, yoghurt and nigella seeds and start binding together. Add the milk, then slowly pour in the yeast mixture, mixing together and kneading into a dough. Add the oil at the end, kneading into the dough. Cover the bowl with clingfilm and set aside to rise for 30 minutes to 1 hour.

Divide the dough into 4 or 5 equal pieces (depending how thin you like your naans) and shape into balls.

Heat a wide, well-seasoned cast-iron skillet or tray in the hot oven.

Using a rolling pin, roll the dough balls out thinly into circles on a lightly floured surface. Place the naans on the hot baking tray and grill for 1–2 minutes until light brown and crispy. Brush with butter and serve immediately.

You can add variations of spices and herbs such as caramelised onions, raisins and garlic.

Makes 4-5

CIABATTA

This recipe requires you to make a sponge the day before. It adds lots of flavour, but crucially gives the dough time to ferment and bubble, giving way to a luscious, light and big-pocketed final bread. Ciabatta dough is very wet and sticky, so it's tricky to handle. Don't worry though – it's supposed to be like this, so don't be tempted to add more flour! If you are really struggling to move it around, dunk your hands in water prior to kneading as the dough won't stick to wet hands.

Ingredients

300ml warm water
7g sachet dried yeast (use
 ½ on Day 1, ½ on Day 2)
400g strong white bread
 flour
40ml olive oil
5g salt

Method

ROASTING - 160-200°C

Day 1: Make the sponge

In a bowl, mix the water with half the yeast and allow to stand for 5–10 minutes so that the yeast can rehydrate properly. You'll see it start to bubble slightly.

In a separate large bowl, mix the yeast mixture with 200g of the flour. Cover the bowl with clingfilm and set aside somewhere cool overnight.

Day 2: Make the bread

A few hours before you plan to cook, add the sponge with the remaining ingredients to a large bowl and mix all the ingredients together well, then knead for 15 minutes. Alternatively, use a food processor fitted with a dough hook on speed 1 for 10 minutes.

Set the dough aside in a covered bowl for about 1 hour until doubled in size.

Tip the dough onto a well-floured surface and cut in half. Transfer to a baking sheet and form into two flat 'slipper' oval shapes. Allow to rise again for 1.5–2 hours.

Slide the bread into the oven and cook for about 20 minutes until golden.

Makes 2 loaves

REMEMBER - KEEP THE OVEN
DOOR CLOSED WHEN BAKING

BLOOMER

Shape this loaf any which way you like – the wood-fired crust spread with cold butter is off the chart!

Ingredients

7g sachet dried yeast

300ml warm water

20ml olive oil

560g strong white plain flour, plus extra for dusting

10g Maldon sea salt

Method

ROASTING - 160-200°C

Mix the dried yeast in a jug with the water and oil and wait 5–10 minutes until it starts to bubble.

Add the flour and salt to a large bowl, then pour in the liquid. Mix all the ingredients together well, then tip out onto a floured surface and knead for 15 minutes. Alternatively, use a food processor fitted with a dough hook on speed 1 for 10 minutes.

When the dough is smooth, return it to the bowl, cover with a tea towel and leave it somewhere warm for about 1 hour until it has doubled in size.

Either place in a proving basket, loaf tin or shape onto a well-floured pizza peel. Cover again and allow to double in size a second time.

Slide into the oven and bake for 25 minutes with the door shut.

Makes
1 Large Bloomer

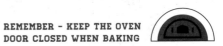
REMEMBER - KEEP THE OVEN
DOOR CLOSED WHEN BAKING

DESSERTS

PEAR & MARTINI TARTE TATIN

A classic dessert with a little boozy twist that's quick to prepare and lovely to cook in the wood oven. Make sure you don't use a non-stick pan when making the caramel.

Ingredients

120g golden caster sugar
6 Conference pears, peeled, cored and cut in half lengthways
40g cold unsalted butter, cubed, plus extra for greasing
40ml Martini rosso
1 pack (320g) of all-butter puff pastry
Crème fraîche, to serve

Method

ROASTING - 160-200°C

Add the sugar to a heavy-based pan on a low–medium heat. Heat the sugar to a nice caramel colour. Keep a close eye on it to make sure it doesn't burn. You can give it a bit of a stir once the caramel has formed.

Reduce the heat to low and add the pears, butter and Martini rosso. Stir it all together and cook for 4–5 minutes. Stir regularly and carefully to make sure all the pears are covered and get a lovely caramel coating.

Roll out the pastry to 3–5mm thick. Have a 20cm pie dish to hand, and cut the pastry into a circle about 2cm larger than the dish.

Lightly butter the dish.

When the pears are ready (they should be tender but still formed), add them to the pie dish one at a time to create a pretty pattern – remember you're working upside down! Then pour over the caramel from the pan.

Place the pastry on top of the pears and tuck the sides down and around the edges of the pears, inside the dish.

Bake for 30 minutes in a wood oven.

When the tarte is done, place a serving dish slightly larger than your pie dish, and quickly turn the pie over. Wear oven gloves and be careful, as the caramel is hot!

Leave to cool for 5 minutes and serve with a dollop of crème fraiche.

Serves
6

SKILLET BROWNIE S'MORES

A quick, simple and fun dessert that's great to present for family and friends to dig in, especially perfect around the campfire. You can also save time and use your favourite shop bought brownies or brownie mixture.

Ingredients

SIZZLING HOT - 220-300°C

FOR THE BISCUIT BASE

6–7 digestive biscuits

50g unsalted butter, plus
  extra for greasing

1 tbsp golden caster sugar

FOR THE BROWNIE

300g dark chocolate

200g unsalted butter

1 tsp vanilla extract

60g cocoa powder

60g plain flour

300g golden caster sugar

1 tsp baking powder

3 eggs

Or . . . your favourite
shop-bought brownies cut
to fit your dish or pan

Pink and white
  marshmallows to cover

Method

Start by making the biscuit base. Lightly grease a 20cm skillet. Get your wood oven to a medium heat and melt the butter in a pan.

Crush the biscuits in a bowl and mix together with the melted butter and sugar. Add the mixture to the skillet, patting down evenly over the base, and cook for about 8-10 minutes.

To make the brownie, break the chocolate up and add it to a bowl with the butter and vanilla. Place the bowl over a pan of simmering water and stir until melted.

Mix all the dry ingredients together in a separate bowl, then add to the melted chocolate.

Beat the eggs in another bowl and add to the mixture, stirring well for a silky consistency.

Pour the mixture over the top of the biscuit base in the skillet and pat down until evenly distributed.

Return the pan to the oven for 20–25 minutes – the centre of the brownie should remain a little gooey.

Dot the marshmallows on top of the brownie and put the skillet back in the oven for about 2 minutes until they are soft and squidgy but still holding their shape. Give everyone a spoon and tuck in!

Serves
6

BAKED CINNAMON APPLES

Ingredients

6 apples, cored

6 tbsp soft brown sugar

2 tbsp ground cinnamon

2 tsp raisins

1 tsp maple syrup

4 tsp mixed nuts

6 tbsp unsalted butter,
  melted

Splash of apple juice

Method

ROASTING - 160-200°C

Stand the apples upright in a shallow dish.

Mix all the remaining ingredients together in a bowl. Fill the cores right to the top with the fruity mixture. Cover loosely with foil and slide into the oven for 20 minutes.

Transfer to a serving platter and drizzle over all the juices from the dish.

Serves
6

CHOCOLATE, RUM & RAISIN BREAD AND BUTTER PUDDING

Super easy to make and always a favourite with the family, this pudding is great eaten cold, but even better hot, with ice cream or cream on the side. You can also experiment with different types of bread, such as brioche or pain au chocolat. You will need to make it 12–24 hours before serving it.

Ingredients

7–8 slices of white bread
4 medium eggs
200g good-quality dark chocolate
50g unsalted butter
100g golden caster sugar
400ml double cream
75ml dark spiced rum
Large handful of raisins
300ml full-fat milk

Method

ROASTING - 160-200°C

Cut or tear the bread slices into quarters. In a 5cm-deep dish measuring about 30 x 25cm, layer the slices of bread so that they slightly overlap and reach almost the top of the dish. Arrange them in a symmetrical or fun pattern if you can.

Whisk the eggs in a bowl.

Set a bowl over a saucepan of simmering but not boiling water. Add the chocolate, butter and sugar to the bowl and stir until melted. Then stir in the cream, rum and raisins. Remove the bowl from the heat and stir in the eggs and milk until the mixture is blended.

Slowly and evenly pour most of the custardy mixture over the bread, making sure to almost cover the bread. Using a spoon, carefully push the bread down to help it soak up all the custard. Repeat the process with the remaining custard. Cover the dish with clingfilm and put a weight on top to help the bread soak up all the mixture.

Allow to cool, then refrigerate (with the weight still on top) for 12–24 hours.

The next day, remove the weight and clingfilm and slide the dish into a medium oven. Cook for about 30 minutes, rotating the dish 180 degrees halfway through cooking.

There are many variations to a good bread and butter pudding . . . the top of this one should be a little bit crunchy.

Serve with rum and raisin ice cream or a generous dollop of cream on the side.

FIG & BLUE CHEESE DESSERT PIZZA

Ingredients

1 pizza base, stretched and
 ready
2 tbsp apricot jam
1 fig, thinly sliced
Small handful of walnuts
75g blue cheese, crumbled
Pomegranate seeds

Method

SCREAMING HOT - 300-450°C

Thinly spread the apricot jam over the pizza base.

Add the fig, walnuts and blue cheese.

When cooked, sprinkle with pomegranate seeds.

Serves
2

BERRY MADNESS DESSERT PIZZA

Marshmallow fluff is wonderful stuff, but it burns in a flash. For this recipe, first cook your pizza base plain then add the toppings and flash back in the oven, keeping a very careful eye on things!

Ingredients

1 pizza base, stretched and ready
3 tbsp strawberry marshmallow fluff
5 strawberries, sliced
5 raspberries, sliced
10 blueberries, sliced
10 mini marshmallows
Strawberry sauce, for drizzling

Method

SCREAMING HOT - 300-450°C

Slide the un-topped pizza base into the oven until cooked through.

Spread the strawberry marshmallow fluff over the pizza base.

Top with the strawberries, raspberries, blueberries and mini marshmallows.

Flash the pizza back in the oven for around 30 seconds.

Drizzle with strawberry sauce.

Serves 1

PAVLOVA

Salvaging beauty from the dying embers.

Ingredients

6 egg whites
330g caster sugar
1 tbsp cornflour
1½ tsp white vinegar
300ml double cream
Fresh berries or fruit of your
   choosing

Method

LOW AND SLOW - 120–160°C

Whisk the egg whites in a food mixer on a high speed until soft peaks form.

Add the sugar, spoon by spoon, allowing it to get worked in before adding more. Whisk for a further 10 minutes until the whites become thick and glossy.

In a small bowl, mix together the cornflour and vinegar, then whisk into the egg mixture for 30 seconds.

Spoon the mixture in a circle onto a greased baking tray and cook in a low oven with the door in place for about 1 hour. If you like, you can leave the meringue in the oven overnight as the oven cools right down.

Meanwhile, whip the cream until it thickens to soft peaks.

When the meringue is completely cool, spread the cream evenly over the top of the meringue and then top with the fresh berries.

Serves
8

PECAN TARTS

Ingredients

FOR THE TART
Sunflower oil, for greasing

150g unsalted butter

200g light brown sugar

2 large eggs

1½ tsp vanilla extract

200g plain flour

2 tsp baking powder

1 tsp salt

100g Werther's Originals
  butterscotch sweets,
  smashed into pieces

150g pecan nuts, roughly
  chopped

FOR THE TOPPING
200ml golden syrup

50g unsalted butter

50ml double cream

¼ tsp Maldon sea salt

60g caster sugar

250g pecan halves

TO SERVE
Vanilla ice cream

Maple syrup

Method

ROASTING - 160-200°C

Start by making the tarts. Lightly grease four 15cm cast-iron skillets with sunflower oil and set aside.

Melt the butter in a dish until it turns a medium-brown colour and has a nutty aroma, around 10 minutes, then remove from the heat, skimming off any scum that forms.

In a large bowl, beat the brown butter and sugar together for 1–2 minutes until combined. Add the eggs, one at a time, beating well after each addition. Beat in the vanilla.

In a separate medium bowl, whisk together the flour, baking powder and salt. Gradually add the flour mixture to the butter mixture, beating until just combined after each addition. Fold in the butterscotch pieces and the pecans. Divide the batter among the prepared skillets and slide into the oven.

Bake for 25–27 minutes until a wooden skewer inserted into the centre comes out clean. Set aside to cool completely.

To make the topping, bring the golden syrup to a simmer in a medium dish for 1 minute, stirring frequently. Remove from the heat, stir in the butter until melted, then stir in the cream and salt.

Allow to cool, then whisk in the sugar and stir in the pecans. Pour the pecan mixture over cooled tarts and serve with vanilla ice cream and a drizzle of maple syrup.

Serves
4

RESOURCES

RESOURCES

DeliVita Pizza Ovens (https://www.delivita.co.uk) Award-winning pizza ovens handmade in Yorkshire by Italians. The ovens are ready to cook in just 25 minutes after lighting them, and – once up to temperature – they can knock out an authentic wood-fire cooked pizza in around 90 seconds. Weighing in at under 30kg, they are portable and can be used on most regular garden-table tops. Plus they look awesome!

Hot Headz Sauces (https://www.hot-headz.com) Stuart and the Hot Headz crew have been importing hot chilli sauces and much more into the UK from around the world for a couple for decades now. This is where to buy the amazing Lizano Salsa you need for making Gallo Pinto, as well as loads besides. Try their Habanero Inferno potato crisps if you dare . . .

Flamers Fire Lighters (https://www.flamersfirelighters.co.uk) Flamers are all natural and eco-friendly. They light your pizza oven (or BBQ for that matter) super efficiently and, because they don't use nasty chemicals, they won't leave a taint on your food.

Thermapen Instant Read Thermometer (https://www.thermapen.co.uk) Thermapen leads the pack when it comes to thermometers. A Thermapen should be your right-hand man when it comes to cooking, as it gives a temperature reading in a matter of seconds, ensuring your food is cooked to the exact 'doneness' every time.

Gränsfors Bruk Axes (https://www.gransforsbruk.com) Another great advantage of owning a wood-fired oven is you get to have an axe. Treat yourself to one that is a pleasure to use. Gränsfors Bruk has been handcrafting axes for over a hundred years. Each axe is signed with the smith's initials. I love them!

Park Tool Pizza Cutter (https://www.parktool.com) I've used dozens of different pizza cutters and always go back to my trusty Park Tool favourite. Park Tool is respected for being an awesome American bike tool company, but randomly it has also turned out to be the best pizza cutter out there. And it looks like a bike, which is cool.

Shipton Mill Flour (https://www.shipton-mill.com) From its online store, Shipton Mill lets you order pretty much any kind of flour you can imagine. It produces all kinds of wonderful organic flour for regular bread making as well as specialist Italian type '00', which is perfect for pizza bases. It also mills flour especially for chapattis or focaccia.

CountryWoodSmoke (http://countrywoodsmoke.com) Marcus Bawdon has built up a terrific resource in CountryWoodSmoke. Find everything from a bank of superb wood-oven and outdoor cooking recipes with how-to videos through to equipment reviews and an extremely lively Facebook community group. Look out for his free quarterly online magazine too!

INDEX

INDEX

Sweet Potato Parmigiana 110

SPHERE

First published in Great Britain in 2018 by Sphere

10 9 8 7 6 5 4 3 2 1

A CIP catalogue record for this book is available from the British Library.

ISBN 978-0-7515-7258-2

Printed and bound in China

Papers used by Sphere are from well-managed forests and other
responsible sources.

FSC	MIX
FSC www.fsc.org	Paper from responsible sources FSC® C104740

Sphere
An imprint of
Little, Brown Book Group
Carmelite House
50 Victoria Embankment
London EC4Y 0DZ

An Hachette UK Company
www.hachette.co.uk

www.littlebrown.co.uk